Global Stage

Literacy Book 6

Paul Mason, Viv Lambert, and Mo Choy

macmillan education

Scope and Sequence

Unit	Reading 1	Reading 2	Reading Skill	Content Area	Social and Emotional Learning	Key Concept	Language Book
Literacy Review	Making Predictions; Sequence of Events; Sensory Details; Synonyms Making Inferences; Understanding the Main Idea and Details; Transition Words						
1 Keep in Touch page 8	**Fiction** *Urgent Message* Story **Literary Term** register	**Nonfiction** *Communication Time!* Informational Text	Understanding Chronology	Science: Technology	Self-Management: Display grit, determination, or perseverance	What are the benefits of communication technology?	**Vocabulary** technology and online safety **Grammar** verbs of thinking, and simple and progressive forms
2 Time for a Change page 24	**Fiction** *My Stay at Camp Karma* Diary **Literary Term** dropped subjects	**Nonfiction** *Why Do We Sleep?* Informational Text	Analyzing and Evaluating	Science: Health	Responsible Decision-Making: Become self-reflective and self-evaluative	Why is it important to have good lifestyle habits?	**Vocabulary** lifestyle and habits, and healthy food **Grammar** present perfect and progressive
3 Dream Big page 40	**Nonfiction** *Communities Making Dreams Come True* Creative Nonfiction **Literary Term** prefix	**Fiction** *Dreams* Poem	Understanding Author's Word Choice	Social Studies: Communities	Self-Management: Exhibit positive motivation, hope, and optimism	Why is it important to have dreams?	**Vocabulary** dreams and ambitions, and persevering to succeed **Grammar** second conditional and *wish* + past forms
4 How's That Possible? page 56	**Nonfiction** *The Sci-Files* Informational Text	**Fiction** *An Enlightening Journey* Fantasy **Literary Term** personification	Making Inferences	Science: Environmental Science	Relationship skills: Prevent interpersonal conflict, but manage to resolve it when it does occur	Why are mysteries so fascinating?	**Vocabulary** facts, mysteries, and illusions, and historical discoveries **Grammar** modals of deduction and obligation: past forms
5 What Is Art? page 72	**Nonfiction** *Cave Painting* Creative Nonfiction	**Fiction** *The Boy Who Drew Cats* Folk Tale **Literary Term** synonym	Recognizing Genres	Arts and Humanities: Art History	Self-Awareness: Identify what triggers own emotions	What would our world be like without art?	**Vocabulary** describing paintings and artistic elements and features **Grammar** past perfect simple and progressive, and narrative tenses

Unit	Reading 1	Reading 2	Reading Skill	Content Area	Social and Emotional Learning	Key Concept	Language Book
6 It's Your Turn page 88	**Nonfiction** *The History of Board Games* Informational Text **Literary Term** antonym	**Fiction** *The Game of Life* Story	Understanding Denotation and Connotation	History: Civilizations	Social Awareness: Respect others	Why do people play games?	**Vocabulary** playing traditional board games and video games **Grammar** indirect questions, and defining and non-defining relative clauses
7 All About Ads page 104	**Fiction** *Commercial Break* Science Fiction **Literary Term** alliteration	**Nonfiction** *Ad Smart* Persuasive Text	Identifying Text and Graphic Features	Social Studies: Communication	Responsible Decision-Making: Discuss strategies used to resist peer pressure	Does advertising influence the way we think?	**Vocabulary** advertising and branding in advertising **Grammar** reported speech
8 What Are the Odds? page 120	**Nonfiction** *Ada Lovelace* Biography **Literary Term** open compound	**Fiction** *The Binary Life* Story	Recognizing Story Structure	History: Computer Science	Responsible Decision-Making: Make decisions based on moral, personal, and ethical standards	Why are numbers important in our lives?	**Vocabulary** numbers, shapes, and symmetry, and statistics descriptors **Grammar** passives
9 Make Up Your Mind page 136	**Nonfiction** *Making Decisions* Instructional Text	**Fiction** *It's Not OK* Story **Literary Term** oxymoron	Identifying Internal and External Conflict	Social Studies: Ethics	Responsible Decision-Making: Reflect on how current choices affect future	How do we handle difficult choices?	**Vocabulary** decision-making and collaborative decision-making **Grammar** third conditional
10 Take the Lead page 152	**Fiction** *Click to Follow* Play **Literary Term** assonance	**Nonfiction** *Recycle Runway* Informational Text	Summarizing Readings	Science: Ecology	Relationship Skills: Resist inappropriate social pressures	How are we influenced by things around us?	**Vocabulary** positive values, and influencing and leading **Grammar** future progressive and future forms review

A Think and write. Predict from the pictures and the title. Where do you think the story is set? Then read.

The Secret Way to Petra

"Hey, there!" said a young boy in long shorts. "Come this way. I can show you a secret way in!"

Zac followed the boy into a cave. It was cool and quiet away from the hot desert sun and the crowds of tourists who were waiting at the entrance to the Lost City. The boy ran off through a long tunnel, jumping over stones and disappearing around corners.

"Wait for me!" Zac's voice echoed.

The tunnel opened out into a narrow passage between smooth pink and red rocks. The boy stopped to show Zac some beautiful ancient carvings in the rock, but then he looked up and smelled the air. "I smell rain!" he shouted and dashed off.

"I didn't know it rained in the desert," said Zac, chasing after the boy. Soon it was raining hard and water splashed around his ankles.

"Up here!" called a voice. Zac looked up and saw the boy sitting high up on a rock. "Hurry! This is an old water tunnel. If it floods, we might drown!"

B Answer the questions. Then discuss how you know.

1 Where do you think the boy in shorts came from?

2 Why did Zac go into the cave?

3 Why do you think this place is called the Lost City?

4 How did Zac feel when it rained?

5 Why was the water splashing around Zac's ankles?

6 What do you think the tunnel was for?

C Read and sequence the events. Then predict what will happen next.

- [ ] The boy climbed up onto a high rock.
- [ ] The boy ran through a long tunnel.
- [ ] It started to rain.
- [ ] Zac met a young boy.
- [ ] He followed the boy into a cave.
- [ ] They stopped to look at ancient carvings.
- [7] ______________________

D Think and write. Then discuss. Complete the table with sensory details from the story. Which sense doesn't have an example?

Sense	Examples
Sight	
Sound	
Touch	
Taste	
Smell	

Literary Term Synonyms

Think and write. What are the synonyms for the underlined words?

~~discover~~ yell simple brothers and sisters

1 If you <u>find</u> a cell phone, you should tell an adult. discover
2 My <u>siblings</u> and I get along really well. ______
3 Please don't <u>shout</u>—I can hear you very well. ______
4 Driving to the store is <u>easy</u> because there is only one road. ______

Now find five pairs of synonyms in the reading.

A Look at the pictures of Machu Picchu. What do you think the big steps are for? Do you think the reading is about the past, the present, or the future?

Machu Picchu

The city of Machu Picchu was built by the ancient Inca civilization in the 15th century. At more than 2,400 meters above sea level, the Inca constructed huge steps in the mountains for farming and making their homes. Their engineering skills were good and they developed ways to transport water to the fields and houses.

Then, in the 16th century, the Incas left the city. They may have died from diseases. Plants grew around Machu Picchu and it disappeared into the jungle. Consequently, this helped to preserve the site. When the Spanish people came to Peru, they didn't find Machu Picchu and it remained hidden from the world. Eventually, in 1911, it was rediscovered by an American historian named Hiram Bingham. About 200 buildings were found around a square.

In order to protect Machu Picchu for future generations, it was named a UNESCO World Heritage Site and is the most visited tourist site in Peru. Some of the buildings have been rebuilt. The area has grasslands, forests, and tropical rainforests, so it's an important area for conservation, too. Machu Picchu must be safely passed on to future generations.

B Read and match the two parts of the sentences.

1 They created steps in the land … (b)
2 Nobody knew about Machu Picchu …
3 It's an important area for conservation …
4 People want to visit Machu Picchu …
5 Some of the buildings have been rebuilt …
6 Machu Picchu became a UNESCO World Heritage Site …

a. because there are lots of different types of plants and animals there.
b. to make it easier to build houses and grow food.
c. to see how the Incas used to live.
d. because it was hidden by the jungle until 1911.
e. to protect it for future generations.
f. to show what they looked like in ancient times.

C Choose one of the three main ideas in the reading and complete the graphic organizer. Write three details for the main idea.

Main Idea	Detail
	Detail
	Detail

D Think, discuss, and write. Why do you think Machu Picchu is a UNESCO World Heritage Site? Write three reasons.

1 ______________________________

2 ______________________________

3 ______________________________

My Reading Journal

What else would you like to learn about Machu Picchu?

I want to learn ______________________________

Literary Term Transition Words

Read and complete.

suddenly **of course** **meanwhile** **as a result** **eventually**

It was a long journey to the coast. ____________, a lot of the children slept on the bus. ____________, their teachers were chatting and planning the trip. ____________ there was a loud noise and everybody woke up. The bus stopped and everyone had to get off. They had a flat tire. ____________ the tire was changed and they got back onto the bus. By the time they arrived at the campsite it was nighttime, so ____________ they had to put up the tents in the dark.

Now find more transition words in the reading.

UNIT 1

Keep in Touch

Think, Pair, Share

A Look at the picture. What is happening? Think about it.

B Discuss with your partner.

I think ...   I think ...

C Share your ideas with the class.

We think ...

D Think and write. What different ways do we communicate with each other? Make a list.

______________   ______________

______________   ______________

______________   ______________

E Read and sequence the events.

- [ ] Finally, the boat sailed out to sea!
- [ ] First, Helen packed her bags.
- [ ] When the boat was loaded, Helen helped Mom to lock up the house.
- [ ] Next, Helen helped her Mom and Dad load the bags on the boat.

Now read **Urgent Message**

Fiction

URGENT MESSAGE

Pia lifted her head off the pillow. Instant message alert. She stared at the clock. 6:00 a.m. *Who could be sending messages this early*? Pia wondered.

Pia looked at her laptop screen. There was the message. But no username or personal information. This was weird. She'd never seen a message without a username before. Pia got up and showed her parents.

"It's a trick," said Dad with a yawn. "Soon they'll ask you for money."

"Never reply to strange messages, you know better than that," said Mom.

"OK," agreed Pia. But she couldn't help feeling a little anxious.

When is it important to reach out to someone?

The second message arrived later that day while Pia was playing a video game online.

No name, no ID. The message gave Pia the heebie-jeebies.

"-oat s-nk"? Pia didn't understand. *Goat stink? Float sank?*

Was the first word boat? Boat sank!

🇺🇸 the heebie-jeebies
🇬🇧 the chills

HELEN: Thursday at 4:50 p.m.

PIA: Thursday at 5:03 p.m.
How's the boat?

HELEN: Thursday at 5:04 p.m.
Great! It's really pretty out here!

HELEN: Saturday at 11:27 p.m.
Isla Garrobo rocks!

PIA: Saturday at 11:30 p.m.
Looks fun!

What online safety rules do you know?

Her friend Helen was on a boat right now, sailing with her parents for vacation. Just the other day, Helen sent Pia some photos. Was Helen in trouble?

Pia knew she shouldn't reply, but she and Helen had a secret code made from the letters of their names. She quickly typed.

Pia needed to be sure.

Words in Context

Find these words in the reading. What do you think they mean?

instant message **weird** **coast guard** **prank** **enlarged**

When she got the message, Pia's heart beat faster. *Phil* was the correct response. It was Helen.

This was no joke. Somehow Helen was sending messages—maybe she still had a phone? But why didn't Helen contact the coast guard? Maybe she couldn't. *Maybe I'm her last chance*, thought Pia.

"Where are you?" Pia typed.

She sat by her laptop, staring at the screen.

Pia needed to do something. She had to find out more, then perhaps she could convince her parents that this wasn't a prank.

What clues do I have? She remembered Helen's family kept their boat at Costa del Sol. *Where were they going? Isla Punta Zacate, wasn't it?*

Pia searched for a sailing map tool online, and found Costa del Sol. Then she found the islands. Using the tools, she drew a line between the two places. The map told her the distance was 154 km.

Pia knew that boats didn't always travel in a straight line, so she circled the whole area. Pia looked at her circle. Helen was stuck somewhere in there. *What did Helen say?* "Small island." On the map there were quite a few. How was she going to find them?

Who is the **protagonist**, or main character, in this story?

The photos Helen emailed me!

Pia opened up the messages from Helen. The last one was sent just two days earlier. It was of Helen sitting on the deck of the boat pointing at a small island. The message said "Isla Garrobo rocks!"

Pia enlarged the map and looked closely at the details. Isla Garrobo, there it was. Helen was on an island between Isla Garrobo and Isla Punta Zacate. Pia drew a smaller circle and studied it. There was only one piece of land inside her circle that made sense. Isla Violín!

Pia grabbed her laptop and ran with it into the living room. She took a deep breath and calmly told her parents everything. She showed them all the evidence she'd collected: the messages, the photo, and the map.

Mom didn't say anything. Then with a nod she reached for her phone and dialed.

"Coast guard, please," said Mom. "It's urgent."

What would you do to communicate if you were stuck on an island?

Explore the Reading

A Answer the questions.

1 When did Pia get the first message? ______
2 Who did Pia's dad think sent the first message? ______
3 What advice did Pia's mom give her? ______
4 How did Pia know Helen sent the messages? ______
5 Where were Helen and her parents stuck? ______
6 Who did Pia's mom call? ______

B Think, write, and discuss. Describe Pia's character. Does Pia remind you of anyone you know? Why?

Pia reminds me of ______ because ______

C Think and write. What different clues and methods did Pia use to solve the problem of the mysterious messages? Make a list.

D Think and discuss. Imagine you're with Helen and her parents on the island. What characteristics would you need to show?

Literary Term Register

Register is the way we speak or write in a particular situation or when communicating with a particular group of people.

Listen. Then think and discuss. What are more formal ways to say the underlined informal words and phrases?

1 <u>What's up</u>? Have you started your homework yet?
2 That car chase in the movie was <u>so awesome</u>.
3 <u>Cut it out</u>! I can't concentrate with all that noise.
4 Just <u>take it easy</u> and don't think about tomorrow.

Now find informal words or phrases in the reading that mean *made Pia scared* and *is amazing*. What other examples can you think of?

A Think and write. Look back at *Urgent Message*. What time did these events happen?

1 Pia remembered where Helen and her parents were sailing from and to. ______

2 Pia received the first message alert. ______

3 Pia's mom phoned for help. ______

4 Pia used a secret code. ______

5 Pia found the island shown in Helen's photo on the map. ______

B Put the events from **A** on the timeline.

Sunrise 6:00 | 8:00 | 10:00 | 12:00 | 2:00 | 4:00 | 6:00 | 8:00 Sunset

2

Chronology is another word for the sequence of events. A timeline is an example of something that uses chronology to list events in the order in which they happened.

C Skim *Communication Time*. Complete the timeline so that the events are in chronological order.

1440s	______
1844	______
______	Nikola Tesla arrives in the United States.
______	Marconi sends a message across the Atlantic.
1969	______
______	The first cell phone call is made.

D Think and discuss. Without modern technology, how would you communicate with people who are far away? How would you make plans?

Now read **Communication Time**

Nonfiction

COMMUNICATION TIME!

Since the earliest days of humanity, communication has allowed people to share ideas, feelings, and thoughts and to exchange information.

People are always looking to improve the way they communicate. Communication technology has grown from the first cave paintings, through the invention of written language, to today's cell phones and wireless internet.

Let's look at some important moments in the history of communication.

How many different ways do you communicate with people each day?

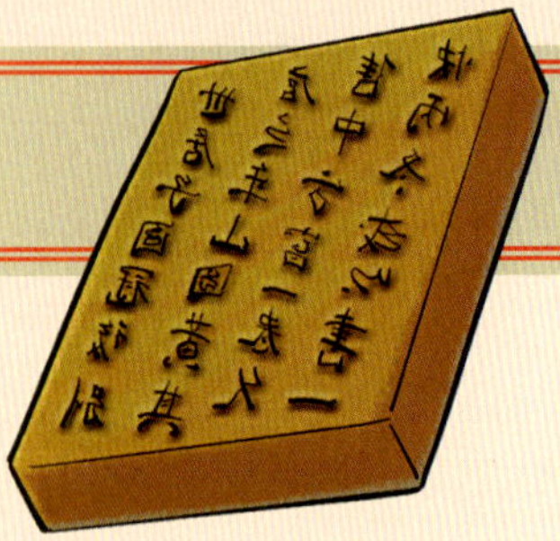

600s The Chinese use woodblocks covered in ink to print on paper.

1440s The printing press is invented. For the first time, copies of books can be made in large numbers.

1844 The first message is sent along telegraph wires by Samuel Morse using his code.

1876 Alexander Graham Bell makes the first telephone call to his assistant: "Mr. Watson—come here—I want to see you."

1890s The radio arrives.

The invention of radio is a big step on the communication timeline. Radio technology provides a way to communicate without wires. People can make easy contact over great distances connecting the world.

Who invented radio communication? There isn't an easy answer.

Guglielmo Marconi VERSUS Nikola Tesla

1895 Italian inventor Guglielmo Marconi experiments with using electromagnetic waves to send signals without using wires. He sends and receives a signal over a distance of 2.4 km.

1899 Marconi sends a signal across the sea between England and France.

1901 Marconi transmits a message across the Atlantic Ocean. The signal is the letter S in Morse Code.

1909 Marconi wins the Nobel Prize. He becomes known as the "father of wireless."

1884 Electrical engineer Nikola Tesla arrives in the United States from Europe.

1890 Tesla succeeds in transmitting energy through the air—the beginning of wireless power.

1894 As a result of his experiments with sending and receiving radio signals, Tesla works out a way to make wireless signals stronger. He patents an electromagnetic coil, known as the Tesla coil, so that no one can copy it and sell it.

1895 Tesla prepares to send a signal over a distance of 80.5 km., but a fire in his workshop destroys all his work.

1898 Tesla plans to build a worldwide wireless system. But his project later runs out of money.

1900 The United States Patent Office recognizes Tesla as the inventor of the radio.

1904 The United States Patent Office reverses its decision and gives Marconi the patent for inventing the radio. (This decision was later reversed in Tesla's favor in 1943.)

Marconi and Tesla built on the discoveries of earlier scientists such as Heinrich Hertz. Radio signals are measured in hertz (Hz).

Words in Context

Find these words in the reading. What do you think they mean?

wireless telegraph patents reverses demonstration wi-fi

While people might argue about who should be known as the real inventor of radio, the story of communication technology doesn't end there …

1906 The first voice and music is transmitted over radio waves. Radio becomes a way of sharing news, information, and entertainment with a huge audience.

Two employees of Marconi were radio operators on the *Titanic* and saved hundreds of lives when it sank in 1912.

1926 John Logie Baird sends a picture wirelessly. This is the first demonstration of television.

1962 The first active communications satellite, *Telstar 1*, is launched.

1969 Scientists create a way of sending messages from one computer to another.

1971 The first demonstration of a wireless computer network happens. This is the early beginnings of wi-fi!

1973 The first cell phone call is made. The world takes a step towards wireless phones!

1989 Tim Berners-Lee creates the World Wide Web, a way of sharing information across the planet. This was the beginning of the internet as we know it.

2004 Online social media service Facebook is launched. It became the first social media site to reach 1 billion users.

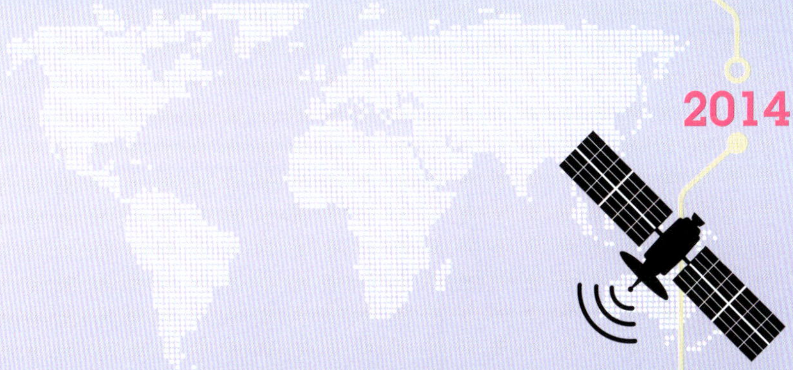

2014 An estimated 7 billion people across the world use cell phones.

2018 Close to 2.7 billion people around the world use social media.

2040 …?

Communication technology has grown since the first words were printed on paper. Scientists and inventors build on ideas that came before.

Communication technology is always changing. What do you think will be next?

How has communication technology changed for you in the past five years?

Explore the Reading

A Read and write *Fact* or *Opinion*.

1. Marconi's inventions were the best. Opinion
2. John Logie Baird's demonstration of television was in 1926. ______
3. Tesla was the world's greatest inventor. ______
4. Television is more fun than radio. ______
5. The first signal across the Atlantic was sent in 1901. ______
6. In 1973, the first cell phone call was made. ______
7. Radio is the world's most useful invention. ______

B Complete the graphic organizer with the main idea and details from *Communication Time*.

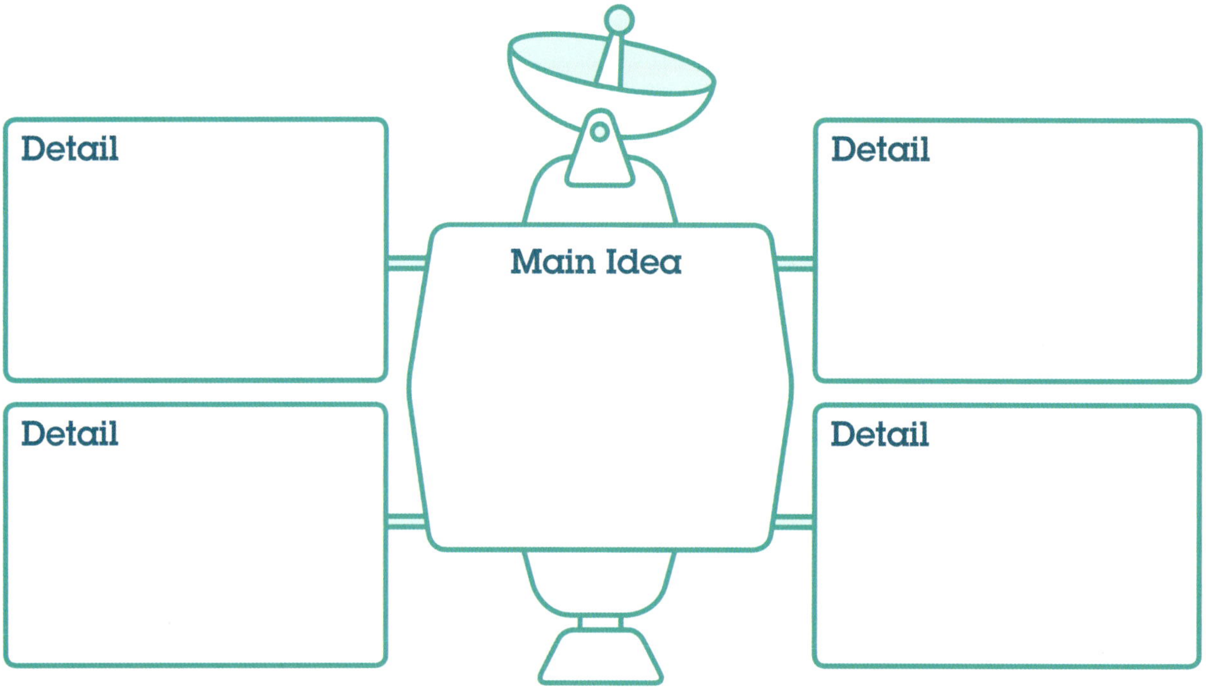

C Think and write. Use the graphic organizer in **B**. Write a paragraph explaining what the reading is about.

______

______

______

______

D Think and discuss. Has communication technology made our lives better? Why or why not?

What are the benefits of communication technology?

A Complete the table. How is communication technology used in *Urgent Message* and *Communication Time*?

Purpose	*Urgent Message*	*Communication Time*
To signal for help		
To get information		
To send messages		
To transmit images		
To entertain		

B Think and write. Do a 5Ws and an H Routine.

Who ____________________?

What ____________________?

Where ____________________?

When ____________________?

Why ____________________?

How ____________________?

Who did you communicate with?

Richard

What did you use to communicate with?

A phone

Where did you use it?

At home

When did you use it?

After school

Why did you communicate?

To invite him over to play soccer.

How did you benefit?

We had a fun time together.

C Look at your questions in **B**. Do a Roundtable.

My Reading Journal

My favorite type of communication is ____________ because ____________

____

A part of the unit I would change is ____________ because ____________

Go back to page 9. **What new thoughts do you have to share?**

UNIT 2

Time for a Change

Step Inside

A Look at the picture. Choose a person or a thing. What can they see?

Let's choose the boy in the blue jacket.

OK, he sees ...

B What do you think they believe?

I think he believes ...

C What do you think they care about?

He cares about ...

D Think and discuss. How healthy is your diet? How often do you exercise?

E Think and predict. Then write. Look at the pictures from *My Stay at Camp Karma*. What do you think happens at Camp Karma?

Now read **My Stay at Camp Karma**

Fiction

MY STAY AT CAMP KARMA

By Cathy Rosales

Sunday, June 27

Excuse my writing! In the car on the way to Camp Karma. Mom's idea of a great family vacation!

How do you think the family might change in their time at Camp Karma?

She says that Dad needs to exercise every day, and that Billy and I have been spending too much time glued to screens and have lost the ability to communicate. As for Mom, she hasn't been sleeping well and is feeling stressed. She got upset when Billy and I started arguing because Billy kept putting his video game in my face! How rude! I'm so stressed I'm biting my fingernails more than ever. Aaargh! I'm dreading it!

Monday, June 28

Survived the first night in our yurt. No, we can't stay in a hotel or a tent like normal people—have to stay in a yurt in the middle of a field! Apparently we'll all sleep better and become nicer people! Mom woke us at dawn for yoga before breakfast. I say breakfast, but there wasn't a sugary cereal in sight, just green smoothies—broccoli and cabbage, cabbage and pear, or broccoli and pear! (Sugar is banned at Camp Karma because it isn't good for you. Billy is NOT happy!) Getting ready for a *gentle* 15 km. hike through the forest with a bunch of other families who are crazy enough to come here.

Words in Context

Find these words in the reading. What do you think they mean?

glued to | fingernails | dreading | meditation | forced to

Tuesday, June 29

Ached all over this morning. Billy and I had a plan. Set off early for the store just outside the entrance to the camp to buy some candy. We were about to escape through the gate when we heard a cheerful "Good morning, kids!"—from Mom and Dad and the Early Bird running group. *Poof* went our plan! Had to join the Early Birds and run around the camp before breakfast! Was so hungry even the green juice tasted good. This afternoon, went to the beach. At last, I thought, a chance to sunbathe! How wrong could I be? Exercising in the sand is even harder than in a gym! I'm exhausted!

What do you think *Poof went our plan!* means?

Wednesday, June 30

They called today a rest day—that meant a morning of chanting followed by meditation. At first Billy and I couldn't stop giggling, but then we closed our eyes and concentrated on our breathing like the instructor said. Afterwards felt unexpectedly happy and calm. Mom and Dad actually smiled at Billy and me over our healthy lunch of fish and green vegetables. We haven't had a nice family meal like that for a long time!

This afternoon we hung out at the yurts. There's no wi-fi so Billy and I were forced to talk to the other weird kids, because there was nothing else to do. Actually had a good time chatting and sharing stories. One of them, Maisie, is really friendly and she can play the guitar, so she played and we sang songs around a campfire in the evening.

Thursday, July 1

No time to write today! Too busy having a wonderful day with Maisie and the gang, hiking to the beach, swimming in the ocean, breathing in the fresh air, and just enjoying being here!

Character arc is how the character changes over time. At the beginning, Cathy is very negative about the camp. How does she feel now?

Friday, July 2

Today was our last day and I hate to admit it, but felt kind of sad. Had our last yoga class on the beach (I'm actually quite good at yoga now!), drank our last smoothies (I asked for the recipes!), and said goodbye to our new friends.

Dad plans to have a daily run, I've stopped biting my nails, Billy has developed a love of broccoli, and as for Mom—she's smiling a lot! Billy and I are going to sing campfire songs all the way home! Goodbye Camp Karma and thank you!

Have you ever been persuaded to do something you didn't want to do and ended up enjoying it?

Explore the Reading

A **Answer the questions. Use evidence from the reading to support your answer.**

1 Why did Cathy's mom want to go to Camp Karma?

2 What did Cathy think of the food at Camp Karma?

3 Why was Cathy disappointed on Tuesday afternoon?

4 What surprised Cathy on Wednesday?

5 Why did Cathy feel sad on Friday?

6 How has the family changed by the end of the week?

B **Think and write. Imagine the week at Camp Karma from Mom's perspective. Write a diary entry for Mom for Friday, July 2.**

C **Think and discuss. Why are vacations good for you? Why is it good to change your routine?**

Literary Term Dropped Subjects

Dropped subjects happen in informal English when we know who the subject is. In diary entries, the pronoun ***I*** or ***we*** is often dropped..

Listen. Circle the dropped subjects.

Hey Maisie, today isn't going well. Billy got up late. He said he couldn't get to sleep last night. We went to school as usual but we got stuck in traffic. I was late for my first class and my teacher gave me an unhappy look. She never asked why I was late. I was so embarrassed! I can't wait for this day to be over. How's your day going?

Now find more sentences with dropped subjects in the reading.

A Think and write. Look back at *My Stay at Camp Karma* and answer the questions.

1 What's your opinion of *My Stay at Camp Karma*? ______

2 What's it about? ______

3 Is it fiction or nonfiction? ______

4 What's the author's purpose? ______

5 How does the author achieve that purpose? What makes you say that?

______

B Think and discuss. Look at your answers in **A**. Think about the information. What's your opinion of *My Stay at Camp Karma* now? Has the opinion you gave in **A** changed?

> Critical thinking involves **analyzing** and **evaluating** texts and not necessarily believing everything we read. In order to do this we have to ask questions about a text such as, ***Who wrote it? Why did they write it? Is it fiction or nonfiction?*** This helps you to analyze ideas and evaluate them by your own set of values.

C Read. Then analyze and evaluate the reading. Answer the questions.

In many countries, school starts at 8:00 a.m., and children who live far away have to get up very early to get to school on time. Research has shown that kids need a lot of sleep and food in order for their bodies to grow and develop. If children don't get enough sleep, they may become ill, have difficulty concentrating in class, or be less successful in class. School should therefore start later—then everyone would be healthier, safer, and happier.

1 What's it about? ______

2 Is it fiction or nonfiction? ______

3 What's the author's purpose? How does the author achieve it?

______

4 Based on your answers, what's your opinion of the reading?

______

D Think and discuss. Read the headings in *Why Do We Sleep?* Do you know the answers to the questions already?

Now read **Why Do We Sleep?**

Nonfiction

WHY DO WE SLEEP?

Why do we sleep? It's a difficult question to answer. We spend about a third of our lives asleep—that's 30 years for a person who lives to be 90—but nobody knows exactly why. Are we wasting our time lying in bed doing nothing when we could be doing something useful? Scientists don't think so. All mammals and birds sleep, even though while they sleep they are easy prey for predators. Fish, reptiles, and insects rest too, so there must be a good reason.

Do you have trouble sleeping on your first night in a new place? Why do you think that might be?

What are the scientific theories?

When we sleep enough we feel better and more energetic; it's easier to concentrate and make decisions. After a good night's sleep, we solve problems and think of new ideas better. We're generally healthier and happier. Scientists have developed several theories for why we sleep.

Our bodies rebuild and replace energy we've used in the day. Muscle grows, tissue is repaired, and hormones, chemicals our bodies need, are produced while we are sleeping.

Our brains recover from the day, store information, and process experiences and memories while we are asleep. Our brains also clear away anything we don't need to remember.

What happens if we don't sleep?

Without sleep, parts of our brains become inactive. We get confused and forget things; we can't concentrate. Tiredness, stress, and difficulty following directions are all results of not getting enough sleep. Also, lack of sleep weakens the immune system, so it can't fight illness very well and we may become sick.

Why do we dream?

When we sleep we may have amazing adventures in our dreams that seem real. We all dream at night, but we don't always remember our dreams. Nobody really knows why we dream, but it might be part of organizing our memories and emotions.

What's the last dream you can remember? Why do you think you had this dream?

Words in Context

Find these words in the reading. What do you think they mean?

hormones **process** **clear away** **weakens** **caffeine** **power nap**

How is modern life affecting sleep patterns?

Before the light bulb was invented, people usually went to bed when it was dark and got up when it was light. In today's world, we go to sleep about two hours later and get up two hours earlier than we used to. Technology has made it harder for us to sleep, so we are more tired. Looking at brightly-lit screens before bed, whether they are TVs, cell phones, or computers, is making it harder for people to get to sleep and harder to wake up in the morning, too.

Why can't I sleep sometimes?

Worrying about something can keep us awake, but there may be several things keeping us from sleeping. Here are a few tips to help:

Don't look at a screen just before bedtime.

Don't eat junk food. Eat a healthy diet, but don't eat just before bed.

Sleep in a cool, dark, quiet room.

Go to bed at the same time every night.

Work out regularly, but not late in the evening.

Don't drink anything with caffeine in it, like soda, coffee, or tea, before bed.

Am I getting enough sleep?

Feeling sleepy or annoyed and having difficulty concentrating and making decisions are signs that we're not getting enough sleep. Most children need between 8 and 10 hours of sleep a night. Keeping a sleep diary noting what time we go to bed, wake up, and how we feel during the day can help us to find out whether we're getting enough sleep. Taking a daytime nap, or a power nap, can help boost energy for studying and playing.

Along with water, food, and oxygen, we also need sleep in order to survive. So falling asleep on the sofa in the middle of the day isn't really lazy. Don't feel bad—instead, consider how much good it's really doing!

Do you sleep well at night? Why do you think that is?

Explore the Reading

A **Underline the part of each sentence that is false. Rewrite that part to make it true.**

1 We spend about half of our lives asleep. a third

2 Most mammals and birds sleep. ____

3 While we sleep, our bodies use lots of energy. ____

4 Our brains do nothing while we sleep. ____

5 There are clear reasons why we dream. ____

6 Looking at screens might help us sleep. ____

B **Answer the questions.**

1 What's the reading about? ____

2 Is it fiction or nonfiction? ____

3 What's the author's purpose? How does the author achieve it?

____

4 Based on your answers, what's your opinion of the reading?

____

C **Complete the table. Look back at *Why Do We Sleep?*. What are the pros of getting enough sleep and the cons of not getting enough sleep?**

Enough Sleep	Not Enough Sleep

D **Think and discuss. Think about people who have unusual sleep patterns. Who are they? How do they get enough sleep?**

Why is it important to have good lifestyle habits?

A Think and write. Complete the table. Look back at *My Stay at Camp Karma* and *Why Do We Sleep?* What do the readings say about these topics?

	My Stay at Camp Karma	*Why Do We Sleep?*
sleep		
food / diet		
exercise		
happiness		

B Think and discuss. What can you change in your own life to be healthier? Do a Three-Step Interview.

C Think and write. What steps could you take to make the changes from **B**?

My Reading Journal

What's the most important information you learned in this unit?

What are some good habits you already have? How did you learn them?

Go back to page 25. **Do the routine again.**

UNIT 3

Dream Big

"If your dreams don't scare you, they aren't big enough."

—Ellen Johnson Sirleaf

3-2-1 Bridge

A Look at the picture. Write three thoughts or ideas you have.

1 __________

2 __________

3 __________

B Write two questions you have.

1 __________

2 __________

C Write a metaphor.

Friendship is like gravity, it holds all things together.

____

D Share your ideas with the class.

E Think and discuss. Dreams don't only happen when we sleep. A dream is also something that we hope for or want to achieve. What dreams do you have?

F Think and write. Look at the headings in *Communities Making Dreams Come True*. What do you think the reading is about?

____

____

Now read **Communities Making Dreams Come True**

Nonfiction

Communities Making Dreams Come True

Cash Flow Problems

Rupa is a hardworking tea farmer in northeast Bangladesh. To help make her business grow, she needed to borrow money.

But Rupa doesn't have a phone or internet access, so she had to go to the nearest bank herself. It took her a day to travel there by bus.

At the bank, Rupa eventually saw someone. Before they gave her a loan, the bank wanted something to guarantee that they would get their money back. Unfortunately, she didn't have anything valuable, so she left empty-handed.

Is it easy for people to achieve their dreams? Why or why not?

Microloans

Rupa was determined to reach her goal, and didn't give up. She heard about organizations giving loans of small amounts of money—microloans—to people who find it difficult to get a loan from a bank. She decided to talk to a nonprofit microloan organization.

What do you think *didn't give up* means?

After carefully assessing her application, the organization loaned Rupa the money she needed. Rupa bought a new tiller, hired two employees to help with the harvest, and was able to pay back her loan on time.

Words in Context

Find these words in the reading. What do you think they mean?

cash flow **nonprofit** **tiller** **campaign** **went viral** **walks of life**

When Noam Tep's fishing nets were stolen, he lost his only source of income, but a microloan meant the Cambodian fisherman was able to make a fresh start by buying some new nets.

Today, there are many organizations working in countries all around the world using microloans to help people achieve their dreams.

Crowdfunding

Siblings Jorani and Leap had a great idea for a game app. Together these Cambodian teens planned all of the levels and figured out that if Jorani drew the characters and backgrounds, and Leap wrote the game to work on cell phones and tablets, they would be onto a winner.

But as soon as they wrote their business plan, they realized they didn't have enough savings to purchase everything they needed. So they turned to a crowdfunding site, offered investors a copy of the game once it was complete in return for their help, and gave themselves a month to raise the money. If they didn't meet their goal, they would delay their plan until they could fund it themselves.

At first, only a few people contributed, but just two days before the deadline, their campaign suddenly went viral! Thousands of people saw their campaign, contributed, and they had all of the money they needed. Jorani and Leap worked really hard and one year later, Octopus Knight was released worldwide!

What do you think *be onto a winner* means?

Crowdfunding is when a large group of people give money to help a particular project or dream become a reality. It's usually done over the internet, where crowdfunding websites connect people with projects and dreams to people who have the money that can help. There are many different websites that help with crowdfunding for a variety of purposes.

In 2014, crowdfunding raised $16 billion for different projects. One year later, this amount more than doubled to $34 billion!

Crowdfunding can be used for artistic projects, such as publishing a book. It can also help raise money for people who need medical help, or for communities who need new equipment or resources.

For more than 20 years LeVar Burton was the host of *Reading Rainbow*, a television show that focused on teaching children about books and reading. In 2014 he launched a crowdfunding campaign on a site called Kickstarter. His dream was to make more *Reading Rainbow* videos, classroom materials, and apps for children all over the world to use for free. The campaign reached its goal in just one day. Today, Burton's dream is real and children everywhere can use the *Reading Rainbow* Skybrary!

What type of business would you start if you had the funding?

Whether it's microloans or crowdfunding, people from all walks of life can use a helping hand to achieve their dreams.

Explore the Reading

A Answer the questions.

1 Why is it difficult for some people to borrow money from a bank?

2 What is a microloan?

3 What is crowdfunding?

4 Where does crowdfunding mostly take place?

5 What did Jorani and Leap offer investors?

6 How long did it take for Burton to reach his crowdfunding target?

B **Think, discuss, and write. Do you think the title fits the article? Why or why not? Write a different title for the article.**

C **Think and discuss. After getting a microloan or donation, what else will someone need to do to make their dream or project a reality? What are ways communities are improved by these dreams and projects?**

Literary Term Prefix

A **prefix** is a group of letters that is added to the beginning of a word to change its meaning.

Think, read, and write. What do you think the prefixes *micro–*, *inter–*, and *un–* mean?

1 The computer <u>micro</u>chip was tiny. *Micro–* means

2 The world's longest <u>inter</u>national flight is from Qatar to New Zealand. *Inter–* means

3 Your room is so messy, it's very <u>un</u>tidy. *Un–* means

Now find more words with the prefixes *micro–*, *inter–*, and *un–* in the reading.

A Read and write. Read the poems. Look at the underlined words. What different words or phrases might the author have used?

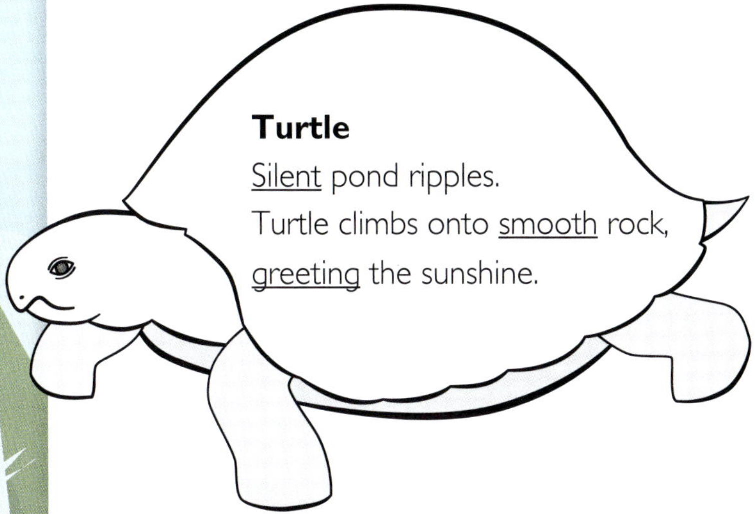

Turtle

Silent pond ripples.
Turtle climbs onto smooth rock,
greeting the sunshine.

1 Silent: ____________

2 Smooth: ____________

3 Greeting: ____________

When we think about author's **word choice**, we look at particular words the author uses in their writing. An author can choose different adjectives to describe something or certain verbs and adverbs to create an effect.

B Look at the underlined words or phrases. Rewrite them using more interesting words or phrases.

1 "You can't go in there," said Jed. ____________

2 Lesley wasn't feeling good. ____________

3 Sophie wore her nice dress. ____________

4 The parrots in the trees were pretty. ____________

5 The bike was new. ____________

6 The old car drove up the hill. ____________

C Think and discuss. How can someone work towards these dreams?

1 If someone wants to score a goal in the next soccer game …

2 If someone wants to become a firefighter …

3 If someone wants to buy an expensive new book …

Now read **Dreams**

Fiction

Dreams

A dream is another way of saying ambition or wish.
It says so in the dictionary.
Something you really want, and hope will happen one day.
A dream. Right there on page 23.

It's tough grasping hold of a dream.
Dreams slip through the air like notes from a guitar,
the ringing of the bell, the whoosh of a roller coaster.
Falling, spinning, floating.

Until they find a home, dreams are almost out of sight.
You need those special dream eyes.
But dreams are there, it's true.
And every dream needs a dreamer.

Faisal dreams of making a stop-motion movie.
He wants to shoot it on his phone
and post it online for his friends. Just for fun.
Super Max to the Rescue!

Faisal paints the scene, and shapes the hero out of clay.
Move, click, move, click! The process takes forever,
but at last it's done! Success!
100 likes already! And it's only been online for a few hours.

Every dream needs a dreamer
with special dream eyes.

What kinds of things do people wish for?

Winning the 100 meters is what Isabel wants most of all.
She's never won before. Third place is her best so far.
Isabel wishes she could feel the string break and know she's won.
She wants a blue ribbon pinned to her chest. But she needs determination.

After school, Isabel stays behind at the track.
She gulps a mouthful of water and starts to dash,
around and around, her legs warming up.
Then she practices her starts: Ready, set, go!

Every dream needs a dreamer
with special dream eyes.

Sofia's dream is for a bedroom, a space to call her very own.
Whisper quiet when she wants to read,
really noisy when she feels like tuning out the world.
She wishes she could paint the walls blue, and have a shelf full of books.

Sofia knows this dream won't happen. Not yet. Not for years.
There isn't a spare room in the house,
not unless you count the closet under the stairs.
But she can dream all the same.

Every dream needs a dreamer
with special dream eyes.

ready, set, go!

ready, steady, go!

Words in Context

Find these words in the reading. What do you think they mean?

stop-motion movie **gulps** **tuning out** **twitch** **hay**

Lilly dreams of snow. She wishes she could feel it, just once.
She wants to lie on her back and move her arms.
Then throw big snowballs at Mom and Dad,
and zoom down a hill on a sled, stopping for hot chocolate.

This poem is an example of **free verse.** Does it rhyme? What else do you notice about it?

Lilly plans a mountain trip: the journey, the clothes, the stay.
She shows her parents. "Can we please, please, go?"
"Maybe," Mom smiles. "If you get good grades at school."
So Lilly works hard. She needs those grades. She wants the happiness of snow!

Every dream needs a dreamer
with special dream eyes.

US	UK
sled	sledge
grades	marks

Seth has a dream. Well, he calls it a goal.
He wishes he had a rabbit. A Flemish Giant—one of the biggest there is.
They have huge ears that stick up, and noses that twitch.
He promises he'll look after it really well.

Seth saves all his money, for weeks and weeks and weeks.
He helps his mother build a big rabbit pen.
They cut wood, pound nails, and fill the bottom with hay.
Then they bring home Buttons. What a happy day!

Every dream needs a dreamer
with special dream eyes.

How do you feel when you accomplish something you've dreamed about achieving?

So you see, you can grab hold of a dream.
It's not always easy, and sometimes it doesn't happen at all.
But like a superhero, a blue ribbon, and a very large rabbit,
it's only impossible if you don't put your mind to it.

Explore the Reading

A **Read and choose the answer.**

1 Dreams slip through the air like notes from a ___b___.

a. song b. musical instrument c. bell d. choir

2 The characters in Faisal's movie are made from ________.

a. wire b. wood c. paper d. clay

3 Winning ________ is what Isabel wants most of all.

a. a game b. a medal c. a race d. a prize

4 Sofia dreams about having ________ bedroom.

a. a spare b. her own c. a clean d. a big

5 Lilly likes ________ weather.

a. cold b. warm c. stormy d. hot

6 Seth wishes he had a ________ Giant.

a. Dutch b. French c. Flemish d. English

B **Think, underline, and write. Underline the verbs in each sentence. Write a synonym for the verb.**

1 It's tough grasping hold of a dream. ________

2 Dreams slip through the air. ________

3 Faisal shapes the hero out of clay. ________

4 Isabel gulps a mouthful of water. ________

5 Sofia feels like tuning out the world. ________

6 Lilly zooms down a hill on a sled. ________

C **Read and write. Look at the first two stanzas of *Dreams*. What are some words and phrases the author uses to describe the ways dreams move and sound?**

Move	Sound

D **Think, discuss, and write. What advice would you give someone who is struggling to achieve their dream? What important characteristics do you need to achieve a realistic dream?**

____

____

Why is it important to have dreams?

A Complete the table. Look back at *Communities Making Dreams Come True* and *Dreams*. What are their dreams? How do they work toward their dreams?

People	Dreams	What They Do
Rupa		
Jorani and Leap		
Faisal		
Isabel		

B Choose a dream you have. Why is it important to you? How can you achieve it? Do a Three-Step Interview.

C Look back at *Dreams*. Use your ideas in **B** to write two new stanzas about yourself.

Your Dream

What You'll Do

Every dream needs a dreamer
with special dream eyes.

My Reading Journal

One thing I will remember from this unit is

Who do you know who might find the information in this unit useful? Why?

Go back to page 41. **Do the routine again.**
How do your new and old responses connect?

UNIT 4

How's That Possible?

Explanation Game

A Look at the picture. Choose a thing. What is it?

Let's choose the sky.

OK!

B What do you notice about it? Tell your partner.

It's yellow there.

And then it turns orange.

C Why do you think it is that way?

Maybe because it's morning.

Or it's ...

D What are some other reasons it might be that way? Share with the class.

We think ...

What do you think?

E Think and write. What real-world mysteries have you heard about? Make a list.

____

____

____

____

F Think, predict, and discuss. Look at the headings and pictures on the next page. What do you think the reading is about? Why do you think it's called *The Sci-Files*?

Now read **The Sci-Files**

Nonfiction

THE SCI-FILES

CASE STUDY 1: Sliding rocks in Death Valley

How can rocks move on their own?

The mystery

The Racetrack is a playa, or dry lake bed, in Death Valley National Park, California, USA. Years can pass without a drop of rain falling here. But it has become famous for a geological mystery. Rocks that are stuck in the dry mud have long tracks behind them. They appear to have moved hundreds of meters on their own.

Possible theories

1 **Hypothesis:** It could have been a trick. Someone might have moved the rocks.

Argument against: They couldn't have done this without leaving evidence of a truck or footprints.

2 **Hypothesis:** Strong winds might have moved them.

Argument against: Many of the rocks are extremely heavy.

What do you think the explanation might be for the two mysteries?

CASE STUDY 1

Investigation

The problem was that nobody ever saw the rocks moving, but a team of scientists had an idea. They fitted rocks with GPS trackers and used time-lapse photography to record any movement. It was going to be a long experiment taking up to 10 years. But only two years later, when scientists visited the site to collect information in 2013, by coincidence, the rocks started to move while they were there. It was icy after some rain and the mystery was solved!

Conclusion

Sometimes rain falls in winter, creating a shallow pond in the playa, half covering the rocks. At night, the temperature drops suddenly. The top of the pond freezes into a thin but strong sheet of ice. On sunny mornings, the ice starts to melt and break up. Light winds cause the floating ice sheets to push the rocks slowly across the playa, leaving tracks in the mud. In spring, the ground dries up and the rocks are left at the end of their tracks.

This rare sequence of events has to happen to start the rocks moving. Because it's dry 99% of the time in Death Valley, this might not happen for many years.

It can take more than 50,000 photos to make a time-lapse video of only 76 seconds.

Words in Context

Find these words in the reading. What do you think they mean?

geological GPS trackers uniform termites colony ecologists aerial

Are these case studies **primary sources** (where the information came from) or **secondary sources** (a description of the primary sources)?

CASE STUDY 2: Fairy circles in the Namib Desert

Where do these amazing patterns in the desert come from?

The mystery

The grasslands of the Namib Desert in Africa are covered with large circles that are uniform in size. They are known as fairy circles and have puzzled the local Himba people for generations. What might have created these bare patches of ground?

Possible theories

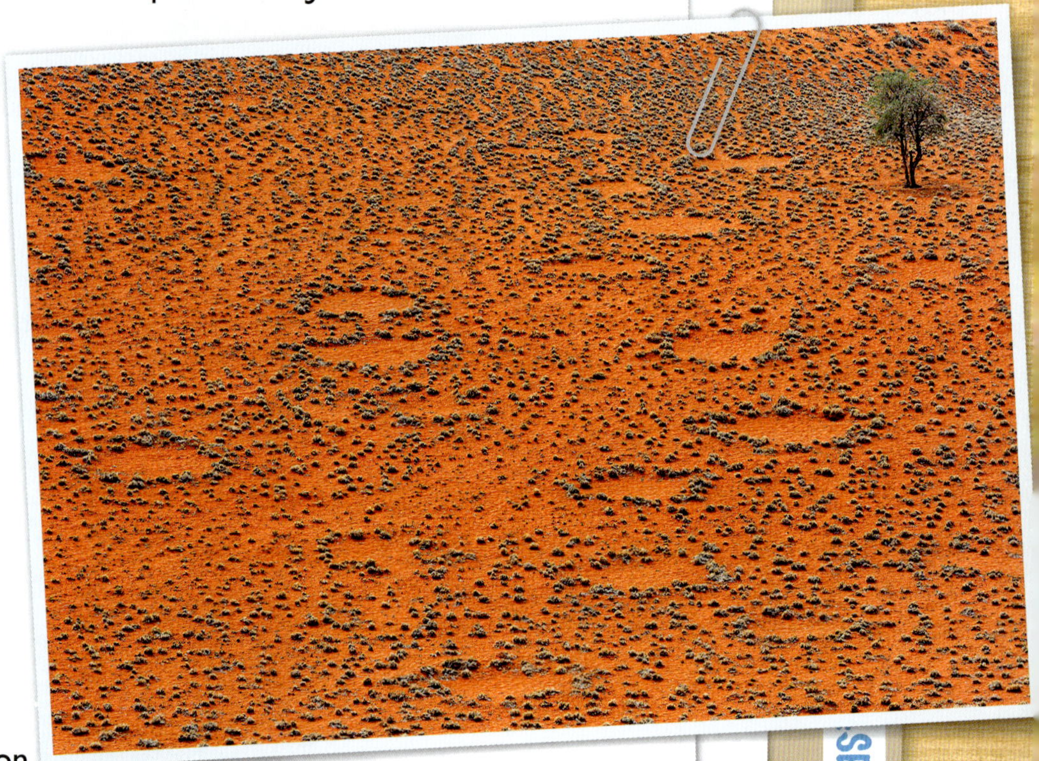

1 **Hypothesis:** Termites were seen in the fairy circles, so the circles might have been caused by termite nests.

Argument against: It didn't explain why the circles are so regular in size.

2 **Hypothesis:** Dying plants might have poisoned the soil.

Argument against: It couldn't have been caused by this as there was no evidence of poison in the soil.

3 **Hypothesis:** Thicker grass grew around the circles, so they could have been caused by plants competing for water.

Argument against: It hadn't been proven by any tests.

Investigation

Termites look for food in a circular area around their nest. If they meet another colony of a similar size, they don't go any further. Ecologists, who study how plants and animals live together, created computer software to investigate the result of termite colonies surrounded by other colonies of a similar size eating the roots of plants above their nests. This caused the plants to die. They also investigated plants living close together that create natural shade for each other but grow long roots. These roots take water from the soil further away, causing the plants there to die. The software predicted regular patterns would be formed of big circles created by the termites eating the plants' roots, and small circles because of the plants competing for water. The team then took aerial photos of the fairy circles.

Conclusion

The aerial photos confirmed the predictions of the software and showed small circles between the large circles. So two of the three theories were correct. Nobody noticed the small circles because everyone was interested in the big circles. They couldn't see the forest for the trees!

forest (US) / wood (UK)

They couldn't see the forest for the trees. What do you think this means?

Explore the Reading

A Think and write. Complete the table.

	Sliding Rocks	Fairy Circles
1 Where does the mystery take place?		
2 What was one of the hypotheses?		
3 What was one of the arguments against?		
4 What technology did they use to solve it?		

B Write *True* or *False*. Then discuss. What makes you say that?

1 It doesn't rain often in Death Valley. ______
2 The mystery of the sliding rocks took the team of scientists a long time to solve. ______
3 It's always very hot at night in Death Valley. ______
4 The Himba people have recently come to live in the Namib Desert. ______
5 Plants develop extensive root systems to search for water. ______
6 The small circles were caused by dying plants poisoning the soil. ______

C Scientists use the Scientific Method to answer a question or solve a mystery. Choose a mystery from **D** on page 57. Complete the diagram with the different stages.

Ask a question

↕

Research the topic
How do you research?

↕

Write a hypothesis

↕

Test the hypothesis
How do you test it?

↕

Make conclusions
What is the result?

A Read and make inferences from the reading to answer the questions. Support your answers with evidence from the reading.

In 1722, a Dutch explorer named Jacob Roggeveen was searching for an imaginary continent called Terra Australis. Instead, he reached a small island in the southeastern Pacific Ocean previously undiscovered by Europeans. He named this extremely remote spot Easter Island. When Roggeveen named it, Easter Island had few trees and little wildlife. The nearly 2,000 inhabitants were expert fishermen and also hunted seabirds. It's believed that 15,000 people were living there only a century before Roggeveen arrived.

1 Did Roggeveen find the place he was searching for?

No, he didn't. He found Easter Island, not Terra Australis.

2 Was the place Roggeveen found the same size as the place he wanted to find?

3 Was Roggeveen the first to discover the island?

4 Why was there so little wildlife on the island in 1722?

When we read, we need to make **inferences** to help us understand a text, because writers don't always provide all the information. These inferences are based on textual evidence and our own knowledge and experience.

B Read and write. Read the introduction to *An Enlightening Journey*. What evidence can you find to support the sentences below?

It was hot and the sun was already high in the sky when Eddy woke up. *A perfect day to take Nora and Josh on another adventure*, he thought. He told Nora about his plan to take them on a boat trip. "Where are we going this time?" asked Nora.

"I haven't decided yet," grinned Eddy, "but we'll need to take lunch and dinner."

1 It's summertime. ____________

2 Eddy often plans adventures. ____________

3 Eddy hasn't finalized his plan. ____________

C Think and discuss. Look at the pictures in *An Enlightening Journey* and think about the title. What mysterious things do you think happen on the journey?

Now read **An Enlightening Journey**

An Enlightening Journey

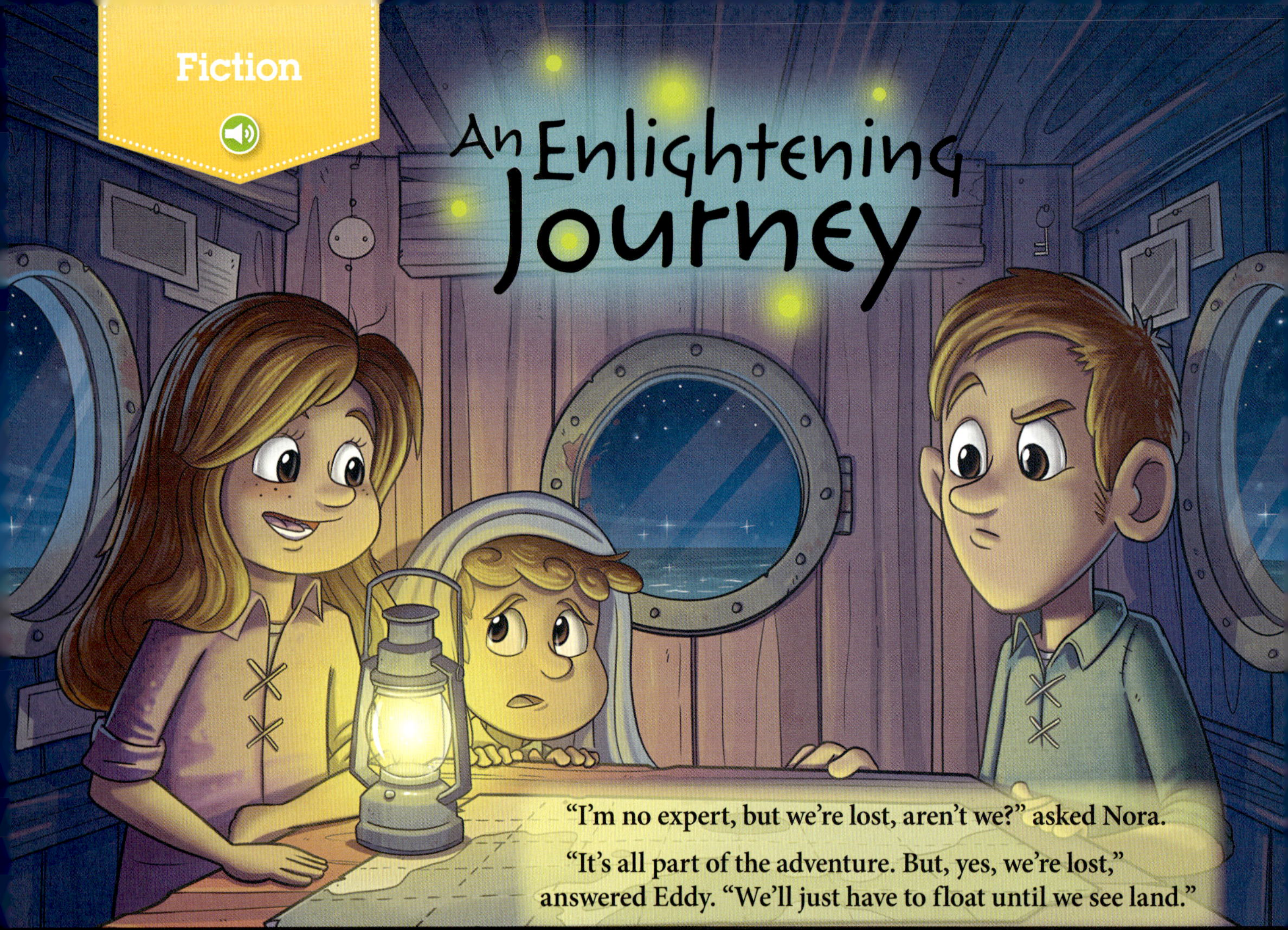

"I'm no expert, but we're lost, aren't we?" asked Nora.

"It's all part of the adventure. But, yes, we're lost," answered Eddy. "We'll just have to float until we see land."

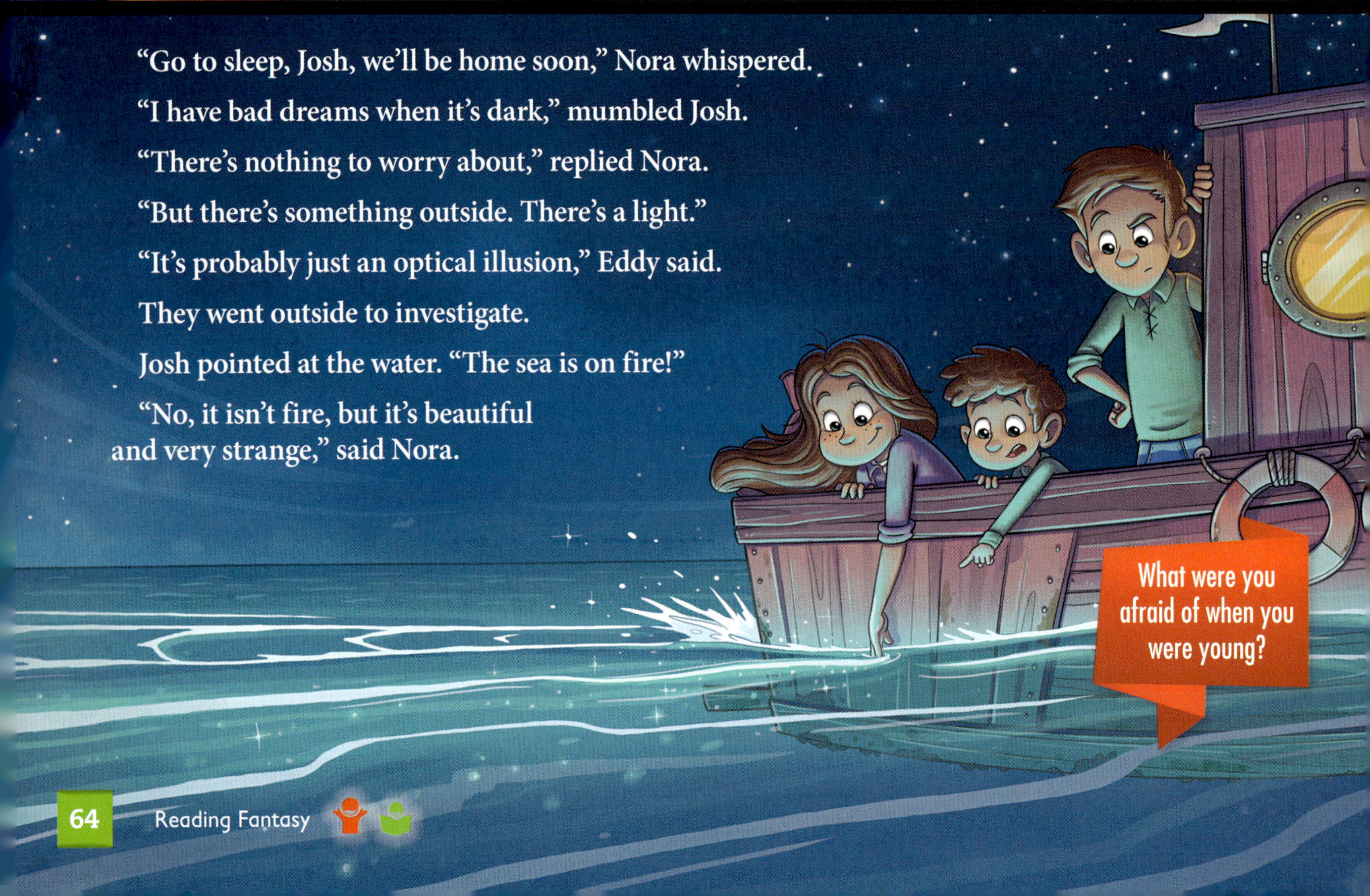

"Go to sleep, Josh, we'll be home soon," Nora whispered.

"I have bad dreams when it's dark," mumbled Josh.

"There's nothing to worry about," replied Nora.

"But there's something outside. There's a light."

"It's probably just an optical illusion," Eddy said.

They went outside to investigate.

Josh pointed at the water. "The sea is on fire!"

"No, it isn't fire, but it's beautiful and very strange," said Nora.

What were you afraid of when you were young?

"I can see land," shouted Eddy suddenly. "Look! That must be a town."

They could hear the sound of thunder in the distance.

Some plants, animals, and bacteria can create their own light, called *bioluminescence*.

"Where's the town?" Eddy was disappointed. "I saw lights. I can't have imagined them. But look at the sea!"

The children watched the sparkling waves dance along the beach.

Josh jumped. "Did you hear that? I think there's something following us."

"No, there isn't, but there's a storm coming," said Eddy. "We should keep moving."

Words in Context

Find these words in the reading. What do you think they mean?

hovered firefly swamp glowing swirling hurling

A single light hovered in front of Josh's face. "What's that? Its tail is flashing."

"It's a firefly," replied Eddy. "Look. There are lots of them!"

As they walked, the ground became softer and wetter.

"I don't like this place. It smells bad," Josh said.

"We're in a swamp, Eddy," whispered Nora.

"I know, but I think we should follow the lights." Eddy pointed to the glowing path. "It's OK, Josh, I'll carry you."

"There's something following us. Listen!" sobbed Josh.

"He's right. I can hear it." Eddy looked up to see a swirling dark shape approaching from the distance. "Run!"

Fireflies light up their tails to attract other fireflies.

“It’s like the monster from my dream!” cried Josh.
The dark shape followed them, pulling trees out of the ground as it chased them through the swamp.
Nora tripped and fell. “Eddy! Help!”
“Get away from her!” Josh picked up a branch and threw it as hard as he could. It swallowed the branch whole.
A crack of thunder and lightning came from the sky as Eddy grabbed Nora’s hand. They ran until they were exhausted.
“A cave. Quick, get inside!” shouted Nora.
Outside, the tornado rushed past the entrance of the cave, hurling branches and pieces of rock in anger.

Inside, the cave was quiet.

"This is unbelievable," whispered Eddy. Looking closely at the strings of light, they could see they were made of threads of silk. "All this must have been made by insects."

Josh felt safe in the cave. "I saved you from the monster, didn't I, Nora?"

"You were very brave, Josh," Nora replied. "You can go to sleep now. Look, the lights are on!"

In the morning, the sun was shining outside.

"Where are you going?" said Nora, rubbing her eyes.

"Now that it's daylight maybe we can find clues to help us get home," answered Eddy. "Let's all go outside."

"We must have walked a long way last night. Just think, we might have been blown away by that tiny tornado!" shuddered Nora.

"But those beautiful lights led us to the cave," said Eddy. "They kept us safe and we only saw them because we got lost!"

"Look. I can see over the whole island. Come on. I have a feeling it's this way. Look, Eddy, Josh, here's a path."

Things felt different that day as they found their way home in the sunshine.

Back home, Nora pulled the blanket up over her little brother.

"Do you want me to leave the light on, Josh?"

"No. I'm not scared of the dark anymore," he answered as he fell asleep.

What are you still afraid of? Have you ever had to face your fear?

Explore the Reading

A **Read and answer the questions. Write evidence from the reading to show how you found your answer.**

1 What was Josh scared of at the beginning of the story?

2 What did Eddy hope to find when they landed on the beach?

3 How did they find their way to the cave?

4 Why wasn't Josh scared anymore at the end of the story?

B **Think and discuss. What do you think really happened? Give a scientific explanation for these mysterious things from the story.**

1 Josh thought the sea was on fire.

2 Eddy thought he saw a town.

3 Josh thought something was following them.

4 Josh thought the black shape was pulling trees out of the ground.

5 Josh thought the lights were on in the cave.

6 Josh thought the creature swallowed the branch whole.

C **Think and discuss. How did the children stop each other from getting upset? Now think of a time you've had a problem. What did you do?**

Literary Term Personification

Personification is when human characteristics or feelings are given to objects, animals, or ideas.

Underline the objects that are personified.

1 The moon hid behind the clouds that cold December night.

2 The sun was shining. The leaves played in the wind.

3 They swam to safety as the sea swallowed the boat whole.

4 Plants are happiest when they have food and water.

Now find more examples of personification in the reading.

Why are mysteries so fascinating?

A Complete the table. What are the explanations for the mysteries in *The Sci-Files* and *An Enlightening Journey*?

Mysteries	Explanations
fairy circles	
sliding rocks	
fire in the sea	
hovering light	
swirling dark shape	
strings of lights	

B Look at **A**. What do all of the explanations have in common?

C Which mysteries in nature fascinate you? Do an Inside Outside Circle.

Why is the sky blue?

D Think and write. Choose questions from **C**. How are you going to find out the answers? Make a list.

My Reading Journal

What stories do you know about mysteries?

Which of the mysteries from this unit did you find most fascinating? Why?

Choose an object from the unit. Then play the Explanation Game.

UNIT 5

What Is Art?

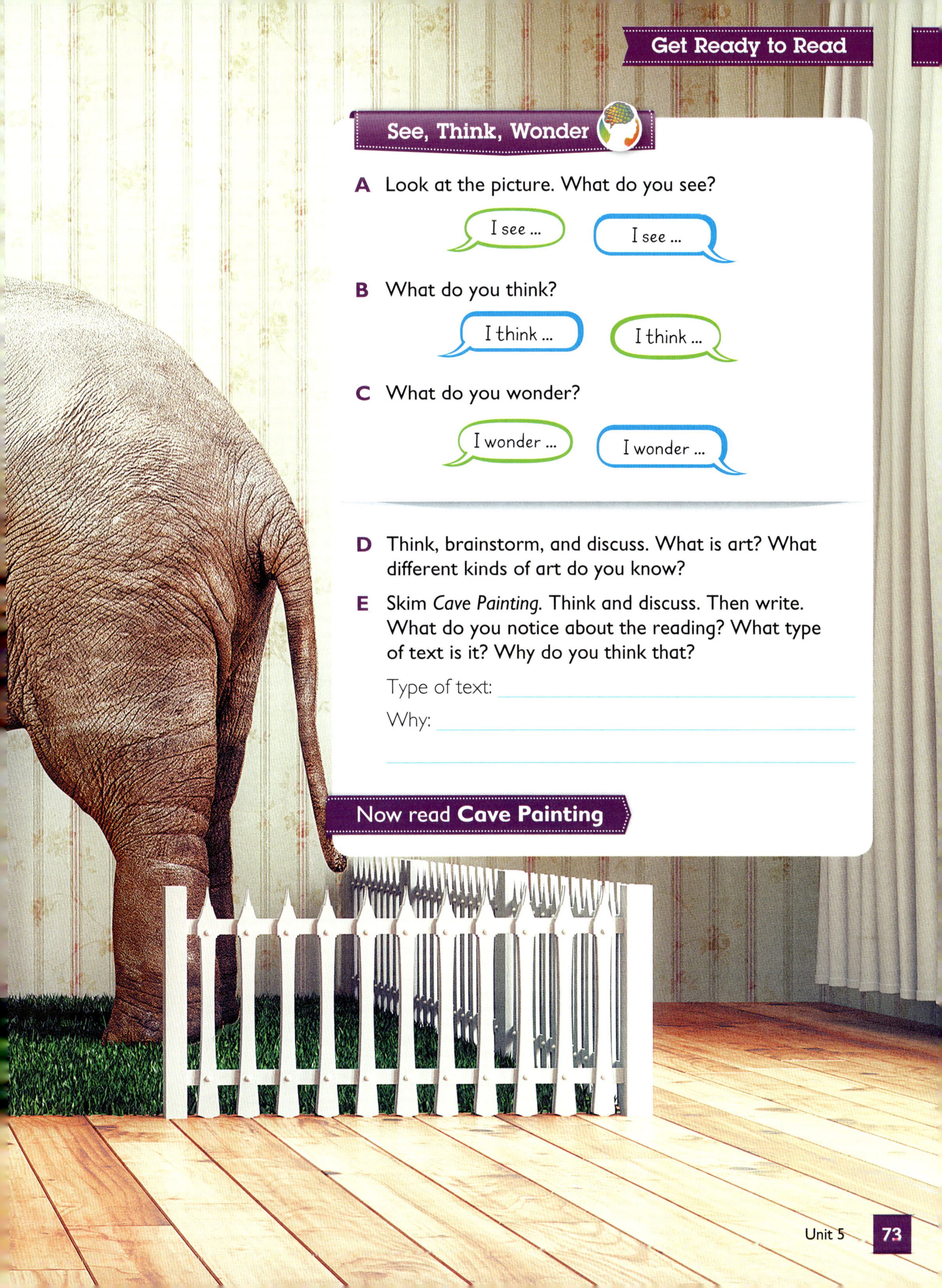

See, Think, Wonder

A Look at the picture. What do you see?

I see ...   I see ...

B What do you think?

I think ...   I think ...

C What do you wonder?

I wonder ...   I wonder ...

D Think, brainstorm, and discuss. What is art? What different kinds of art do you know?

E Skim *Cave Painting*. Think and discuss. Then write. What do you notice about the reading? What type of text is it? Why do you think that?

Type of text: ____________________

Why: ____________________

____

Now read **Cave Painting**

Nonfiction

CAVE PAINTING

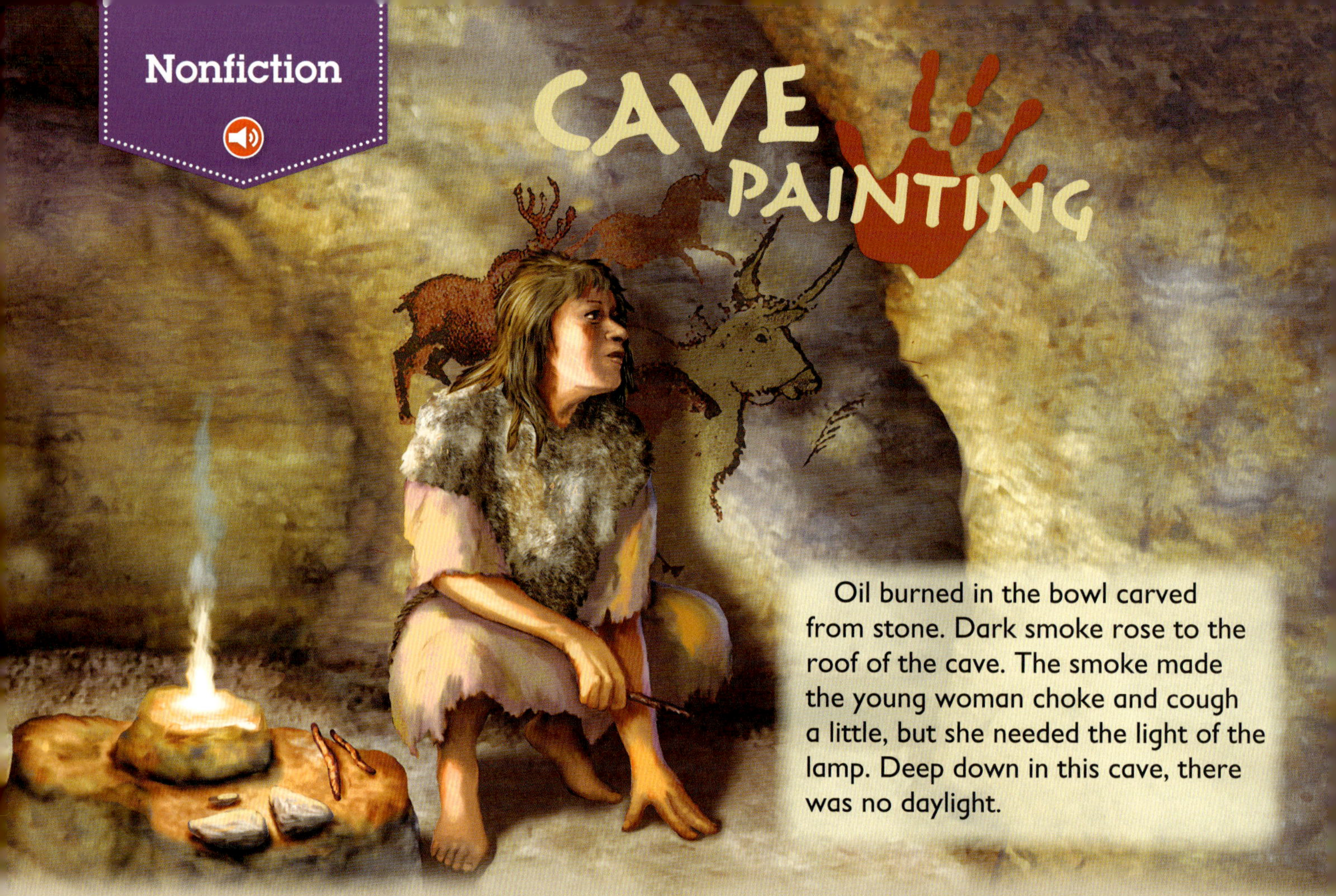

Oil burned in the bowl carved from stone. Dark smoke rose to the roof of the cave. The smoke made the young woman choke and cough a little, but she needed the light of the lamp. Deep down in this cave, there was no daylight.

The artist had laid out her tools the day before: pieces of charcoal she'd saved from the fire, flint, twigs, and tiny bones. She stared at them and the cave walls. Her paintings covered the cave with giant bulls, deer, and horses. This spot was still empty, ready for a new piece of art. What would she paint?

To recreate the art made in a cave 15,000 years ago, today's artists can work with digital tools. Instead of a cave wall and charcoal, there are design programs and styluses.

To begin working, the digital artist switches on her desktop computer and monitor. The artist opens up Illustrator, a design program, and makes sure her drawing tablet is connected.

Next, she creates a new file and saves it as cave_painting.ai.

Why do you think early humans used caves for their paintings?

The artist picked up a piece of charcoal. She began to draw simple lines, a few squiggles. With a thicker piece of charcoal she sketched some powerful shapes, the neck of the horse and the dark mane. When she liked what she saw, she smudged the lines with her finger to create shadows.

With the file ready to use, the digital artist touches her stylus to the tablet and selects a brush tool. She chooses its thickness. She starts with a thinner brush type.

Next, pressing gently, the artist moves the stylus over the surface of the tablet. The stylus acts and feels just like a pencil. On screen, the artist follows her stylus strokes as she sketches the outline of the horse.

If the artist makes a mistake, there is also an eraser tool that can correct any errors.

Now that the outline is finished, she selects some of the shapes and applies a filter—this creates a smudge effect that matches the messy lines of the original.

Does the word *filter* here mean an object that removes solids from liquid; or a digital effect that changes the way the image looks?

Words in Context

Find these words in the reading. What do you think they mean?

charcoal **recreate** **stylus** **tablet** **smudge** **strokes** **slider**

She wanted to choose a color for the horse's body. She had painted many of her animals in black or charcoal. She wanted this one to stand out, so she chose a contrasting color, something brighter than all the other animals. The woman found her powdered red clay, and mixed it with some water, adding more powder to get it just right. Then, with a brush she had made from horsehair, she started painting.

The digital artist opens up the color picker in her program. To get the red of the cave paint, which came from iron oxide, the artist uses the slider tools to mix red, green, and blue.

With the color chosen, a few more touches and the shape of the horse is filled with red.

Iron oxides are chemical compounds, or mixtures of chemicals. They can be used to make paints.

The artist smiled. *Now this wall is finished.*

Just one more thing. She filled a hollow bird bone with red paint. She put her hand on the wall beside her art. Then she blew into the bone, spraying the paint over her hand and onto the wall. When she lifted her hand, an outline of her hand was on the wall.

Her print was next to the horse, for everyone to see.

The drawing stage complete, the artist finds a photograph of a rock surface similar to the cave wall. She opens the photo file and with a few touches she adds her horse drawing to the rock surface. She moves the horse until it's in the best place. It looks like it's painted on rock.

At last, the digital cave painting is finished. The artist saves her file. She posts it in an online gallery, beside a photo of herself. Now, her work is shared for everyone to see.

Explore the Reading

A Think and write. Choose the word or phrase that matches the definition.

horse-hair brush | **file** | **monitor** | **stylus** | **oil lamp** | **slider** | **charcoal** | **flint**

1 Something made from burned wood ______

2 A computer screen ______

3 A hard, gray stone ______

4 An instrument for marking on a computer ______

5 A light that you can carry ______

6 A set of information on a computer ______

7 An object used for painting, with a handle and bristles ______

8 A control on a computer that can be moved from side to side ______

B Compare and contrast the cave painting and today's digital art. Complete the Venn diagram.

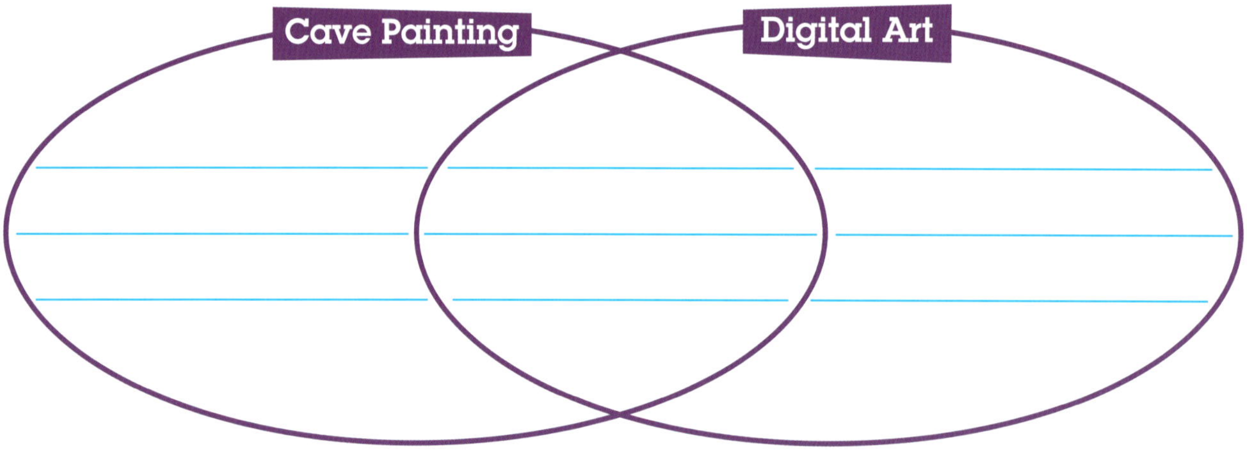

C Think, discuss, and write. What do you notice about the way the author organized the reading? Why do you think they did that?

______

______

D Think and discuss. Why did people want to paint all those years ago? Why did they need art?

A Read, think, and write. What genre are these readings? Why do you think that?

1 *An Enlightening Journey*

"It's like the monster from my dream!" cried Josh.

The dark shape followed them, pulling trees out of the ground as it chased them through the swamp.

Nora tripped and fell. "Eddy! Help!"

"Get away from her!" Josh picked up a branch and threw it as hard as he could. It swallowed the branch whole.

Genre: ______________________

Why: ______________________

2 *Communities Making Dreams Come True*

LeVar Burton was the host of *Reading Rainbow*, a television show that focused on teaching children about books and reading for more than 20 years. In 2014 he launched a crowdfunding campaign on a site called Kickstarter. His dream was to make more *Reading Rainbow* videos to post online, classroom materials, and apps for children all over the world to use for free.

Genre: ______________________

Why: ______________________

Each of the many different **genres**, or kinds of writing, has its own features and purposes. When we try to decide what kind of genre a piece of writing is, we look for clues or language features.

B Label the features that are in *Urgent Message* with a U. Label the features that are in *Communication Time* with a C. Then discuss which genre each reading is.

1 not real ____
2 contains facts ____
3 is real ____
4 has dialogue and narration ____
5 has characters ____
6 has dates ____
7 has a plot ____
8 talks about real people ____

C Think and discuss. Skim *The Boy Who Drew Cats*. What genre is it? Why do you think that?

D Think and discuss. Think of a story that is the same genre as *The Boy Who Drew Cats*. Describe it briefly.

Now read **The Boy Who Drew Cats**

Fiction

The Boy Who Drew Cats

A RETELLING OF A JAPANESE FOLK TALE

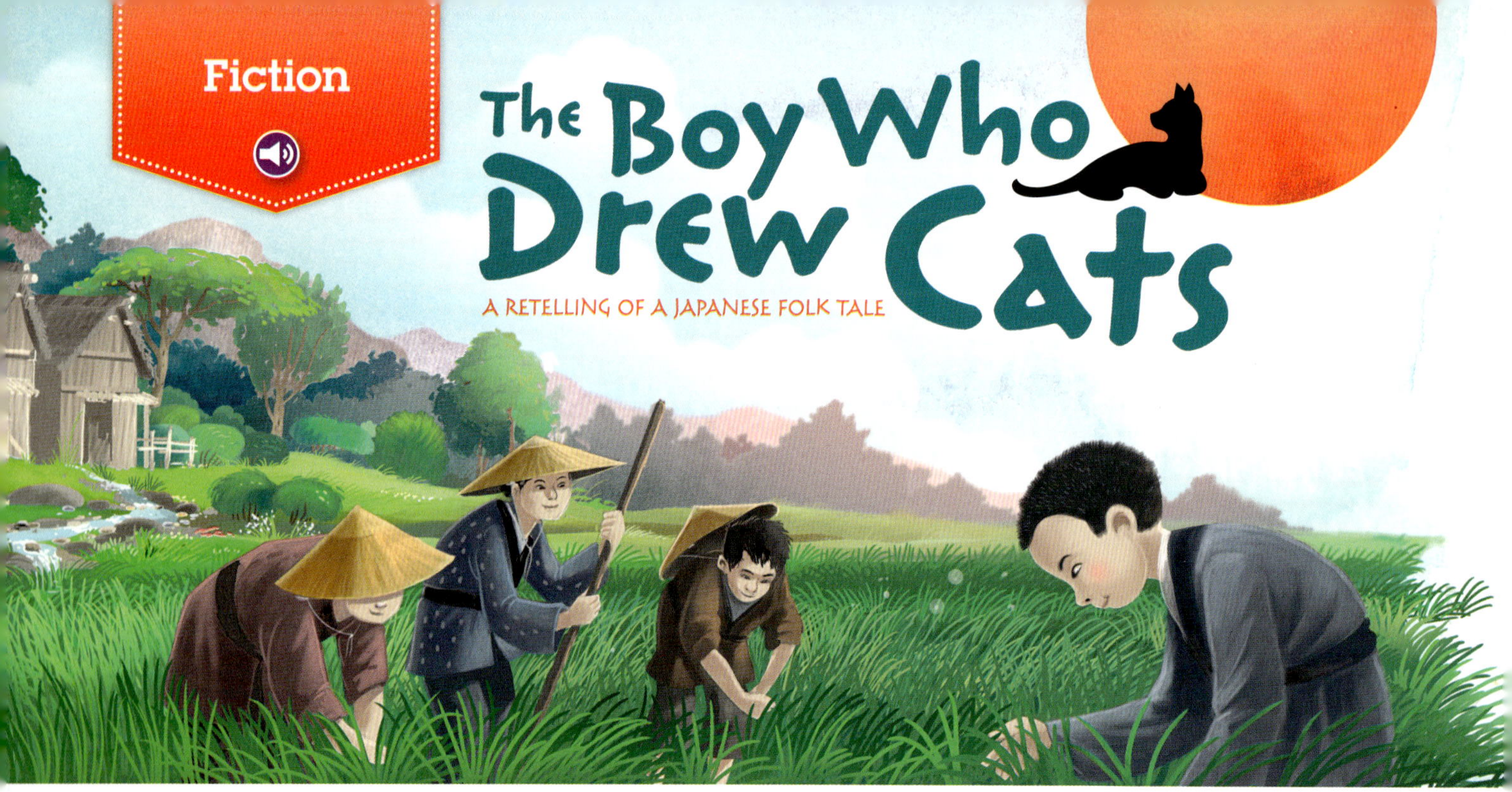

Long ago, in a small village in Japan, there lived a family of farmers: the father Takeshi, the mother Aki, and their four sons.

Three of Takeshi's sons followed in their parents' footsteps and sweated beside them harvesting rice. But the youngest son had no interest in farming.

His name was Jun, meaning "obedient" in Japanese—that means doing as you are told. But when Jun went to the fields, he spent most of the day drawing in the dirt with a stick. Drawing made him happiest of all.

How do people feel when they make art?

Jun drew cats. Big cats and little cats. Enormous cats and tiny cats. He drew old cats and kittens. There were tabby cats with stripes like a tiger and cats with curious eyes.

"What are we going to do with him?" grumbled Takeshi.

"He's been drawing since he was a toddler. He never stops," Aki said desperately.

"Send him to Hideaki the Wise," suggested the villagers.

Hideaki had taught the emperor himself! So Jun went to study with Hideaki the Wise.

Hideaki tried to teach Jun to write in the old style, and to read the great books. But Jun was only interested in art. When he sketched, it made his heart sing. Drawing made him feel free.

"See this cat, Master Hideaki," said Jun. "Look how it has a tail like a snake and ears like mountain peaks."

"I've failed," sighed Hideaki.

Hideaki returned Jun to his parents after just a week.

Words in Context

Find these words in the reading. What do you think they mean?

swarms **scurrying** **rakes** **beasts** **fled**

That winter, a cold wind blew. Snow had been falling for weeks on end, covering the countryside like a quilt. But the frosty wind did more than freeze the bones of the villagers. It drove hundreds of rats from the fields into the village.

The rats came in swarms seeking somewhere warm to hide. They tore holes in the walls and ate the grain in the village stores. They stole rice from the kitchens and chewed holes in socks. The villagers didn't know what to do.

Only Jun didn't seem bothered. With the ground covered in snow, he started drawing his cats on the walls, using pieces of charcoal from the fireplace.

When Jun ran out of room on the walls of his home, he sketched cats on the walls in the village. Huge cats and small cats, striped cats and spotted ones.

Jun's cats soon spread all over the village. His art covered every wall.

"Jun's cats are so playful, so free," said the villagers, smiling.

They forgot about their problems for a while. But the villagers weren't the only ones to notice Jun's cats.

Foreshadowing is when the author gives hints or clues to something that is going to happen later in the story.

One day, there came a terrible thunderstorm that made the ground tremble and shiver and shook the rats from their hiding places.

Scurrying from place to place, the rats looked up and froze. There above them, an army of giant cats was staring down at them. Monstrous cats with sharp teeth like daggers and claws like rakes.

The rats saw there were cats in the grain store and cats in the marketplace. There were cats in the kitchen, cats in the baker's, and cats in the butcher's. They were surrounded by cats!

The rats squeaked in terror. It was better to be cold than to be caught by giant beasts. With one last look at the terrifying creatures, they fled back into the countryside as fast as they could.

"Jun's cats!" cried the villagers. "They've saved us!"

The very next day, Takeshi and Aki bought a book of drawing paper, a brush, and a pot of ink. From then on, they left Jun to draw as much as he wanted.

And it will come as no surprise that he was happy.

Do you prefer to communicate by drawing, writing, or speaking?

Explore the Reading

A Read and choose the answer.

1 Which brother is Jun?

a. oldest b. middle c. youngest d. only

2 What did Jun use to draw cats in the dirt?

a. his finger b. charcoal c. a stick d. a brush

3 What was Jun's teacher called?

a. the Intelligent b. the Wise c. the Strong d. the Clever

4 What did Jun's heart do when he sketched?

a. shouted with joy b. laughed c. sang d. beat faster

5 What didn't the rats eat?

a. socks b. grain c. rice d. bones

B Think and write. How does the author of *The Boy Who Drew Cats* describe these things?

1 Tabby cats' stripes ______

2 A cat's tail ______

3 The snow ______

4 Cats' sharp teeth ______

C Think and discuss. What activity makes you really happy? What makes you excited or scared? Why?

Literary Term Synonym

A **synonym** is a word that has the same meaning as another word.

Write the synonym for each underlined word.

minor hilarious positive pretend

1 The movie we saw last night was <u>funny</u>. ______

2 Our stories were all <u>made-up</u> and silly. ______

3 Some of the details were <u>unimportant</u>, so we didn't read them. ______

4 They studied hard, so they were feeling <u>optimistic</u> about their grades. ______

Now find three pairs of synonyms in the reading.

What would our world be like without art?

A Compare and contrast the artists from *Cave Painting* with Jun from *The Boy Who Drew Cats*. Complete the Venn diagram.

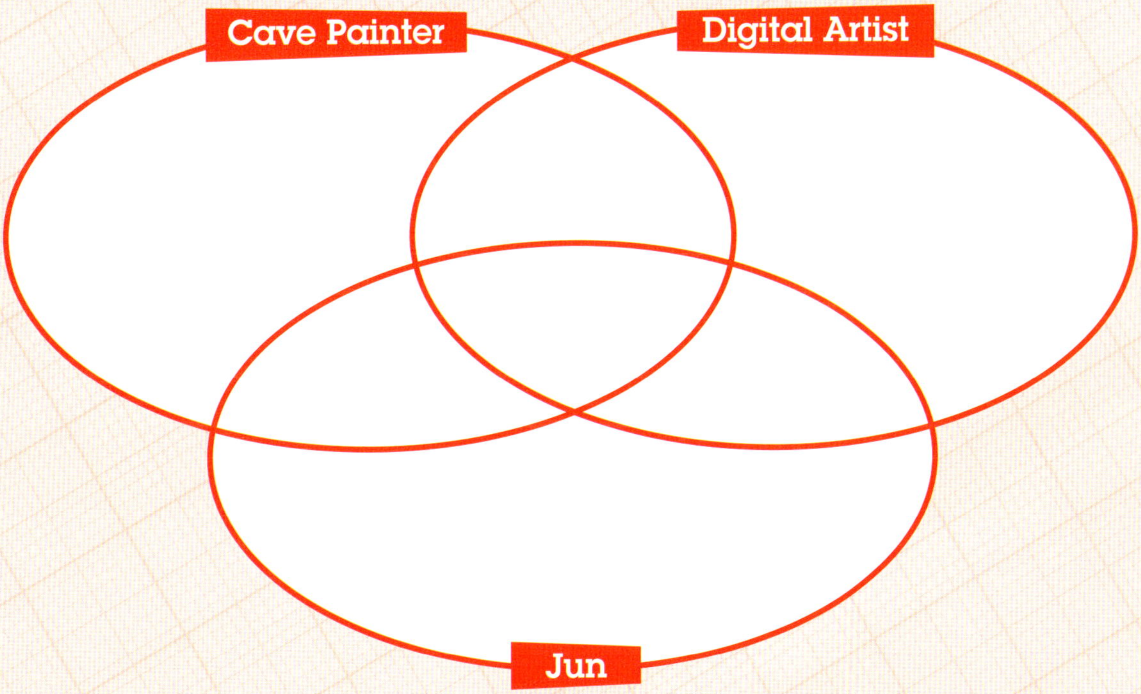

B Read and think about the questions. Then discuss with your group. Do a Four Corners routine.

Corner 1: Why do people create art?

Corner 2: What are the benefits of art?

Corner 3: How would the world be different without art?

Corner 4: How have the technology and tools for making art changed over time?

C Share your group discussion with the class.

My Reading Journal

One question I have after reading this unit is …

Who do you know that would enjoy this unit? Why?

Go back to page 73. **What new things do you see, think, or wonder?**

UNIT 6

It's Your Turn

Question Starts

A Look at the picture. Then brainstorm questions. Write a list.

Who · What · Where · When · Why · How

B Look at your list from **A**. Which questions seem most interesting? Discuss them with the class.

How does virtual reality work?

Are they together?

C What new ideas or questions do you have now? Talk about your ideas with your partner.

When will virtual reality be part of everyday life?

Is his character rich?

D Think and discuss. What games do you play?

E Read and underline. Choose the words or phrases that you think make the paragraph sound more positive.

On a **stormy** / **rainy** day on the weekend, there's nothing I like more than staying **at home** / **in the house** and **relaxing** / **being lazy**. I often **ask** / **invite** some **friends** / **people I know** to come and **play** / **join in** a board game with me. Sometimes we choose **an uncomplicated** / **a simple** game like checkers. Other times we want something more **challenging** / **complicated**, like chess. Whichever game we choose, we always **like it** / **have fun**.

Now read **The History of Board Games**

Nonfiction

THE HISTORY OF BOARD GAMES

As the famous author Roald Dahl said, "Life is more fun if you play games." Go, chess, Snakes and Ladders, and many more board games have been enjoyed all over the world for centuries by people old and young. New games are designed all the time, but traditional games have been part of our cultures for thousands of years and are one of the oldest forms of social interaction. Let's have a look at the history of board games!

Which of the board games in this reading do you know?

Archaeologists have found painted stones and bones that might have been pieces from early board games. These games existed before we had written language! Even the Ancient Egyptians enjoyed escaping from daily life by playing Senet—a set of this early board game was found in Tutankhamun's tomb. There is no record of the exact rules, but it was a kind of race across a grid between two players and it may have inspired the game of backgammon.

Go was invented in China more than 2,500 years ago. The rules of this ancient game with black and white pieces are simple, but the game is challenging and requires discipline and strategic thinking in order to carefully plan each step. People still play Go today and after all these years, the game has hardly changed.

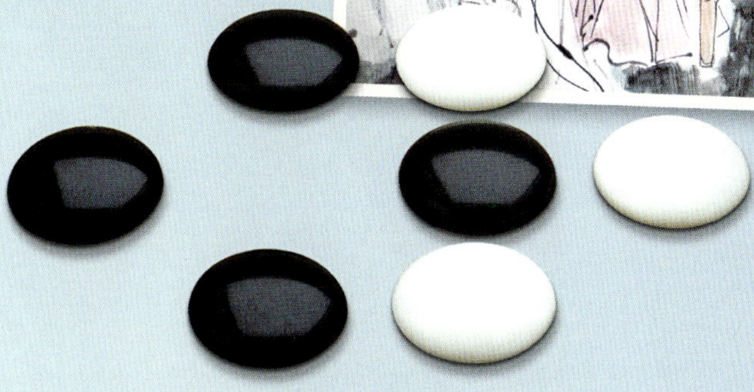

AlphaGo, a computer program, beat the three-time European Go champion Fan Hui in an amazing scientific breakthrough in 2016.

Early games of chess were played in India hundreds of years ago, but the pieces were different from those we recognize today. Instead of castles, bishops, knights, and pawns, there were elephants, horses, chariots, and soldiers. Today, over 600 million people play chess and there are tournaments all around the world. Chess requires concentration, as well as logic and strategic thinking. It may also help us to plan ahead and to search for solutions to our real-life problems.

Words in Context

Find these words in the reading. What do you think they mean?

grid strategic thinking pawns gracefully intricately

Many board games teach us life skills, such as communicating, following rules, taking turns, and, most importantly, learning how to win and lose gracefully. Snakes and Ladders was originally used to teach important life lessons. The ladders represented positive things people might do, while the snakes represented the negative ones. This reflects the fact that although great things might happen to us in real life, there will also be disappointments. We also learn more than just vocabulary and spelling when we play Scrabble, which requires us to be patient and wait our turn, and the real estate game of Monopoly may even help us to spend our money more wisely.

Today, games like Trivial Pursuit and Pictionary are on the shelves of most board game lovers. Whether players are good at geography, history, art, or science, there are questions for everyone in the general knowledge game of Trivial Pursuit. Creative types enjoy playing Pictionary, in which teammates try to guess what image is being drawn.

Perhaps inspired by the interactive worlds of video games, more modern games involve imaginative settings and intricately designed boards with wonderful details. In Catan, the beautiful board represents an island. Players compete for resources to build cities and roads to colonize the island.

For people who don't like competition, there are cooperative games like Pandemic or Forbidden Island. Instead of competing with other players, everyone must collaborate to win these games. In Pandemic, players work together traveling between cities treating diseases, discovering cures, and building research stations. Forbidden Island has a team of adventurers racing to collect treasures before the island sinks under the sea.

Do you prefer board games or video games? Why?

In these days of digital gaming, it may be surprising that sales of board games are increasing, but many games are timeless as well as ageless. Families and friends still love getting together to move plastic pieces around a piece of cardboard. Perhaps, like the ancient Egyptians, we enjoy the face-to-face interaction and friendly competition that they offer. So, come on everybody, Roald Dahl was right—let's have some fun and play a game!

Explore the Reading

A Read and choose the answers to complete each sentence.

1 Two ancient board games are ________ and ________ .

a. Senet b. Pandemic c. Monopoly d. Go

2 Pieces were originally made of ________ and ________ .

a. plastic b. bones c. cardboard d. stones

3 Senet was played by ________ .

a. the king b. the emperor c. the pharaoh d. the queen

4 In Snakes and Ladders, the snakes represent ________ .

a. long journeys b. challenges c. bad behavior d. being lost

5 Pandemic and Forbidden Island are ________ games.

a. competitive b. computer c. cooperative d. ancient

B Write *True* or *False*. Then discuss evidence from the reading.

1 Games have always been played for social reasons. ________

2 It's easy to win at Go. ________

3 Chess hasn't changed since early times. ________

4 Trivial Pursuit and Pictionary aren't very popular. ________

5 Modern board games have taken ideas from digital gaming. ________

6 Cooperative games are ideal for people who want to win. ________

C Think and discuss. What are the traditional board games in your country? Compare and contrast them to the games in the reading.

Literary Term Antonym

An **antonym** is a word that means the opposite of another word.

Underline the antonyms in each pair of sentences.

1 I borrowed your book last week. It was nice of you to lend it to me.

2 These shoes are expensive. You can buy two cheap pairs for the same money.

3 It's dangerous in a thunderstorm. You should stay inside where it's safe.

4 If you're sick, go to a hospital. They'll help you get healthy again.

Now find four pairs of antonyms in the reading.

A Complete the table. Look back at *The History of Board Games*.

Meaning	Paragraph	Word or Phrase in the Reading
Played	1	enjoyed
Getting away from	2	
Give ideas for	2	
Difficult or complicated	3	
Players on the same team	6	
Not competitive	8	
Kind and pleasant	9	

Words or phrases can have two kinds of meanings. The **denotation** is the dictionary definition of a word. The **connotation** is an additional idea or emotion associated with a word. Some words have positive or negative connotations, which sets the tone of the text and elicits certain feelings in the reader.

B Read, think, and discuss. Look at the underlined words and phrases. Which have a similar meaning? Explain how each word or phrase has a positive or negative connotation.

SuperSoccer is an interesting new video game where you enter a fascinating and original world in which extraordinary players, like wolves and robots, compete to win the international Kingdom Cup. Choose your favorite player and 10 teammates and then play against other teams online. The feature players like most is being able to talk to other competitors on the SuperSoccer Forum—it's great for making friends all over the world as you chat, share unusual tips, and all kinds of other useful information.

C Think and discuss. Have you ever played online multi-player games? How did you feel about playing with others?

Now read **The Game of Life**

Fiction

THE GAME OF LIFE

Why do you think some people are unkind to others?

goalie (US)
goal keeper (UK)

Words in Context

Find these words in the reading. What do you think they mean?

headset **tackled** **bully** **forum** **opponent** **tactics**

Conflict in a story is a struggle between two opposing forces. In this story there are two types of conflict: external conflict and internal conflict.

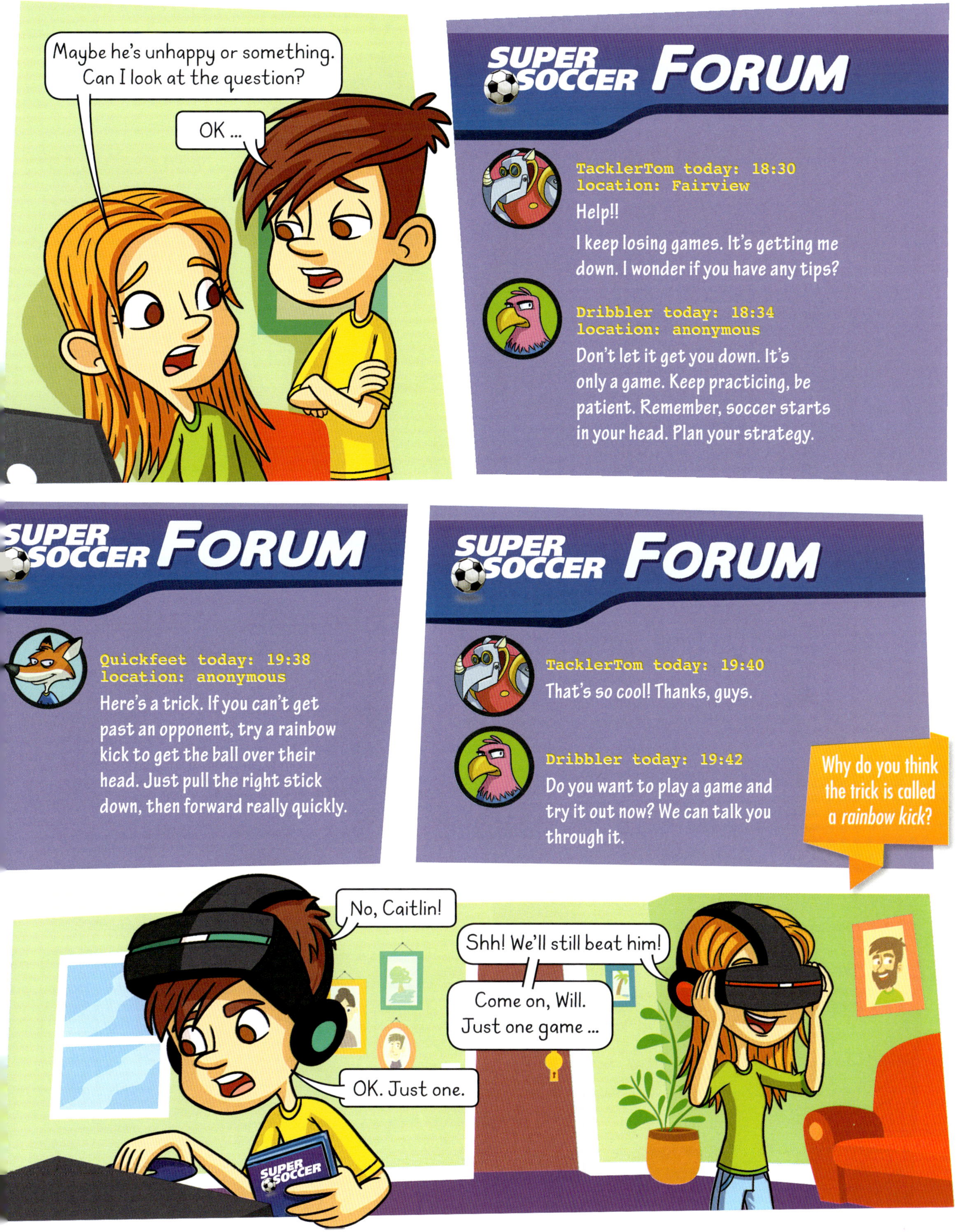

Why do you think the trick is called a *rainbow kick*?

Stop! You can't score from there. Take your time and pass the ball like in a real game.
How about trying a rainbow kick to get past that defender?
Good try, but you weren't fast enough ...
Tom kept trying ...
That was great!
It's five-nil to the pink team! Amazing tactics.
Yes!

Dad? Want to kick a ball around after dinner ... if you have time?
Sounds good, but I promised your mom I'd take the dog to the park ...
Maybe we could take the ball to the park, too?
Actually, that's a great idea! We can go together.
The next day at soccer ...
Great goal! Wait a second ... was that a rainbow kick?
Yep! I learn a lot playing SuperSoccer.
I visualize what my player does in the game, then copy it in real life. Soccer starts in your head, remember?
Dribbler?
No, that's my sister. I'm Quickfeet! Pleased to meet you, TacklerTom.
Come on, let's win this game together.
What lessons can you learn from video games?

Explore the Reading

A Answer the questions.

1 How is Tom mean to Will in the story?

2 Why does Tom play SuperSoccer every evening?

3 How does Will find out that he and Caitlin have been playing SuperSoccer against Tom?

4 What do you think Caitlin means by "soccer starts in your head"?

5 Why do you think Tom suddenly asks his dad to kick around some balls?

6 Why does Tom think Will is Dribbler?

B Think, write, and discuss. Write whether the underlined words and phrases have positive (*P*) or negative (*N*) connotations. Discuss why.

1 Just … stuff at home. ____

2 I barely touched you! ____

3 OK. Just one. ____

4 Amazing tactics … ____

C Think and discuss. Other than Caitlin, who else could have recognized that Tom was unhappy? What could they have done about it?

D Think and discuss. Which of these statements do you agree with? Why?

1 You shouldn't say something online that you wouldn't say to someone's face.

2 You should double-check what you've written before you send or post it.

3 Some things you write could be misunderstood or might sound mean or rude.

4 It's OK to say anything on social media because you can hide behind your username.

5 You should write kindly and remember the other person reading your message.

6 You don't need to be polite on social media.

Why do people play games?

A Complete the table. What do *The History of Board Games* and *The Game of Life* say about these topics?

	The History of Board Games	*The Game of Life*
Playing games for social interaction		
Playing games to escape		
What players learn from games		
Playing games for enjoyment		

B Think and discuss. Look at **A**. Do *The History of Board Games* and *The Game of Life* have similar messages? Why do you think that?

C What different types of games do you play? Do a Think, Pair, Share. Make a list.

D Think and discuss. Do you prefer cooperative or competitive games? Why?

My Reading Journal

How did the readings in this unit make you think differently about games?

Can you recommend a game, a video about games, or a game strategy?

Go back to page 89. **What new questions do you have?**

UNIT 7

All About Ads

3-2-1 Bridge

A Look at the picture. Write three thoughts or ideas you have.

1 ______

2 ______

3 ______

B Write two questions you have.

1 ______

2 ______

C Write a metaphor.

______

______

D Share with the class.

E Think and write. Where do you see advertising? Make a list.

______ ______

______ ______

______ ______

______ ______

F Think and discuss. Look at the pictures in *Commercial Break*. What kind of reading is it? How can you tell?

Now read **Commercial Break**

Fiction

COMMERCIAL BREAK

Science fiction allows us to consider the potential consequences of our current technology choices.

Cassie leaned against the bus window and stared out at the streets. As she watched the city go by, messages flashed across the lenses of her Insta-Glasses.

The bus drove past an airline office, and Cassie's glasses told her that she should "book a flight now." In the park, the trees said: "Love your park. Don't be lazy, grab your garbage!"

Cassie stared at the advertisement that popped up when they passed Go Shoes.

"Great, I want some tennis shoes," said her brother Frank, looking at the ad.

Cassie hadn't thought about it, but maybe she did need some new shoes.

A new message suddenly popped up on Cassie's lenses. "See you this weekend for bargains. Share this message with your friends for 20% off! Great. Grand. Go Shoes." Cassie blinked and selected her friends. She blinked again. Message sent.

garbage
advertisement

rubbish
advert

How can you escape advertising?

As the bus pulled up to their stop, Cassie stared at the ads covering the school building. At the same time, she tried to read the news headlines running down the side of her lenses.

Cassie took off her glasses and rubbed her eyes. Lately, all these messages were giving her a headache. Why did everything need to be covered with ads all the time?

Cassie looked around, making her eyes wide. It actually felt good with the Insta-Glasses off. Things looked different. *Why not?* thought Cassie. With a shrug, she put the glasses in her bag.

Words in Context

Find these words in the reading. What do you think they mean?

lenses **popped up** **lockers** **squinted** **distracting**

"Thanks for sharing the message about the shoe sale," said Eva when she spotted Cassie at the lockers. "Hey, where are your glasses?"

"I figured I'd switch off for the rest of the day," said Cassie.

"A whole day?" said Frank. "No way!"

"You'll be so out of touch," Eva laughed.

Frank asked her how she would get her news and messages.

"It's just till my headache goes away," said Cassie.

"Of course, sure," said Frank.

In science class, Mr. Daunt was teaching about how cats' tongues work. Cassie stared at the photo on the screen.

Mr. Daunt pointed at the screen. "If you zoom in with your glasses, you'll notice the whitish area is actually rows of backwards-facing barbs made of the same stuff as your fingernails."

Cassie looked around the classroom. Her classmates had all zoomed in on the photo, the little red lights on their glasses blinking. She squinted at the photo, trying hard to see what they saw, but couldn't see what Mr. Daunt was talking about. Cassie realized that there was no zoom feature when you just used your eyes.

"That tongue looks like my hair," laughed Frank, making the class giggle.

"Focus on the lesson," said Mr. Daunt.

Are there laws or organizations in your country to make sure advertising is fair?

In art class after lunch, Cassie had fun with a paintbrush. It felt good to hold the brush in her hand. She dripped and swirled paint over her paper, making patterns. The colors seemed so bright, so alive.

“Check out my painting,” she said to Eva.

“You should see what I’m doing with mine,” replied Eva. She adjusted her glasses.

“But you haven’t even picked up your brush yet,” said Cassie.

Eva shrugged. “I’m using a painting app. Same thing.”

Cassie thought that it wasn’t the same. But she didn’t say anything.

“The latest Skate Duty album is on sale—my favorite band!” said Eva, her glasses flickering.

On the ride home after school, Cassie sat beside Frank again.

"How's the headache?" her brother asked.

"It's gone, thanks," said Cassie.

"You should put your glasses back on," said Frank. "I'm watching a trailer for the new *SuperSoccer* movie."

Cassie shook her head and stared out the window. As they passed the park, she saw the bright, white swans on the lake. She hadn't noticed them floating there that morning. But now there were no distracting messages to get in the way. *Everyone should try this*, thought Cassie.

Before Frank could stop her, Cassie reached over and took off his Insta-Glasses.

"Time for a commercial break," she said.

How do you feel about advertising?

Explore the Reading

A Answer the questions.

1 Which advertisement has an environmental message?

2 Why does Cassie share the shoe store ad with her friends?

3 How do Insta-Glasses help everyone keep up to date?

4 What excuse does Cassie give for not wearing her Insta-Glasses?

5 When does Cassie miss her Insta-Glasses?

6 Why does Cassie prefer painting to using a painting app?

B Think and write. What are the pros and cons of wearing Insta-Glasses? Make a list.

Pros	Cons

C Think and discuss. Would you go offline like Cassie, even if all your friends were online? Why or why not?

Literary Term Alliteration

Alliteration is the use of the same letter or sound at the beginning of different words in a sentence, especially in poetry.

Listen and say. Underline the letters or sounds that are the same.

1 Peter Piper picked a pickled pepper.

2 Five fat flamingos flew fast.

3 Round the rocks the rascal ran.

4 I used to yearn for Europe in my youth.

Now find more examples of alliteration in the reading and pictures.

A Think and write. Look at the excerpt from *Communities Making Dreams Come True.* What text and graphic features can you see?

Microloans

Rupa was determined to reach her goal, and didn't give up. She heard about organizations giving loans of small amounts of money—microloans—to people who find it difficult to get a loan from a bank. She decided to talk to a nonprofit microloan organization.

After carefully assessing her application, the organization loaned Rupa the money she needed. Rupa bought a new tiller, hired two employees to help with the harvest, and was able to pay back her loan on time.

1 ______________________

2 ______________________

3 ______________________

4 ______________________

Text and **graphic features** are words and pictures that stand out on the page. **Text features** are things like titles, headings, and captions. **Graphic features** are things such as drawings, graphs, or diagrams.

Text and graphic features make the reading look more interesting, but also make the reading easier to follow and understand.

B Check (✔) and write. Which of these text and graphic features can you find in *Ad Smart*? Write any other text and graphic features you can see.

◯ Heading	◯ Infographic	◯ Chart
◯ Title	◯ Sidebar	◯ Bold
◯ Caption	◯ Callout	◯ Italics
◯ Photograph	◯ Illustration	◯ Text

____

C Think, discuss, and write. Is advertising aimed at children a good thing? Why or why not?

____

____

Now read **Ad Smart**

Nonfiction

AD SMART

What different kinds of advertising are there?

Three busy cities, three different countries, three different languages. What looks the same?

A child is watching TV. The cartoon suddenly stops. Now the child is learning about the latest toy.

For homework, a student finds a website with good information. Messages about a book she searched for earlier flash on the side of her screen.

The judges in a TV talent show are all drinking the same brand of soda.

A character in a movie eats at a popular fast-food restaurant.

What do all of these have in common? They're all forms of advertising.

Advertising to children

Advertising helps raise awareness about a product, business, or service. Today, advertising is everywhere.

Research shows that the average child in the USA sees about 16,000 television commercials a year. That's almost 45 a day! That's not counting the ads on the internet, ads on billboards, ads in magazines, commercials on the radio, or commercials at the movie theater. Even while watching a movie, there's probably product placement, when companies pay to have their products in movie scenes.

153 = Number of hours of television an average person in the USA watches in a month

In fact, it is thought that companies spend about $17 billion each year advertising to children.

Why? Children and teens often have their own money to spend, and they also affect the way their parents spend money. This spending power is worth hundreds of billions of dollars a year.

Why is this an issue?

Some people argue that children younger than eight aren't old enough to understand that ads are selling something. Really young children might find it difficult to tell the difference between a commercial and a TV show because they look and sound the same.

Researchers argue that many ads for children promote junk food using cartoons. This encourages them to buy unhealthy foods, which can add to health problems. This is one example of how advertising can influence the values children are developing at this age.

For these reasons, many countries have rules about advertising for children. In some countries, like Sweden and Norway, there are bans against advertising to children under the age of 12.

Words in Context

Find these words in the reading. What do you think they mean?

service **product placement** **spending power** **catchy** **cookie**

Advertising techniques

Advertisers have many different ways to persuade people to buy or do something.

Repetition: A customer is more likely to buy a product the more times they have seen the advertisement. This is why advertisers repeat their ads.

Association: An ad might also use catchy slogans or phrases that people will remember.

Endorsement: Some advertising will use a favorite cartoon character or a celebrity to help sell their product or service.

Promotion: An ad could also offer a discount, free gift, or say that people can save money.

Emotional Appeal: An ad might suggest that the audience will be happier if they buy the product. An ad could also make the audience sad or scared to encourage them to do something.

Which of these advertising techniques have you noticed?

Internet advertising

Advertisers have different internet tools. For example, when someone visits a website, the website can put a small file on their computer called a cookie. A cookie stores information about how that person uses the internet. Cookies track what sites the person uses, what information they search for, and what things they like.

The next time the person goes online, advertisers can show them ads based on that information. These are called targeted ads.

But advertising can be put to good use, too. To do their work, many charities and community groups depend on donations from the public.

Advertising allows these groups to raise important issues, show the problems they are trying to solve, and tell people about the opportunities they are providing. They can tell stories of people they have helped. They can ask the public to donate money to support their work.

What can children do to be ad smart?

When looking at an ad, consider what the ad is really saying.

Which company is behind the advertising?

Who do they want to sell the product to? Who is this ad for?

What does the ad want the viewer to think or do?

Which technique is the ad using?

Are you ad smart? Why or why not?

When children think critically about ads, they see which parts of the ad don't make sense to them or are not true for them. Then they can make better choices about which products they buy or ask their parents to buy. In a world full of advertising, it certainly pays to be ad smart.

Explore the Reading

A Write three questions about the reading to ask a partner. Trade and answer your partner's questions.

Question 1: ____________________

Answer: ____________________

Question 2: ____________________

Answer: ____________________

Question 3: ____________________

Answer: ____________________

B Think and discuss. Why do some countries have rules about advertising aimed at children?

C Think and discuss. Why did the author write *Ad Smart*? How does the author achieve that purpose?

D Think and write. What advertising techniques do you see in the ad?

E Think and write. Do you think advertisements are a necessary part of daily life? Why or why not?

Does advertising influence the way we think?

A Complete the table. List the advertising techniques in *Ad Smart* and examples of these advertising techniques in the pictures and text in *Commercial Break*.

Advertising Techniques in *Ad Smart*	Examples in *Commercial Break*
Repetition	the ads the children see on the bus
Slogans	

B Think, discuss, and write. Your class is going to hold an event to raise money for charity. Do a Roundtable. Complete the table.

Type of Event	Types of Advertisements	Techniques
	1	4
	2	5
	3	6

C Think and write. Look at **B**. Write an advertising slogan to persuade people to come to your event using one technique you discussed.

My Reading Journal

Which of the text and graphic features did you find useful in the unit? Why?

Who do you think might learn something by reading this unit?

Go back to page 105. **Do the routine again. How do your new and old responses connect?**

UNIT 8

What Are the Odds?

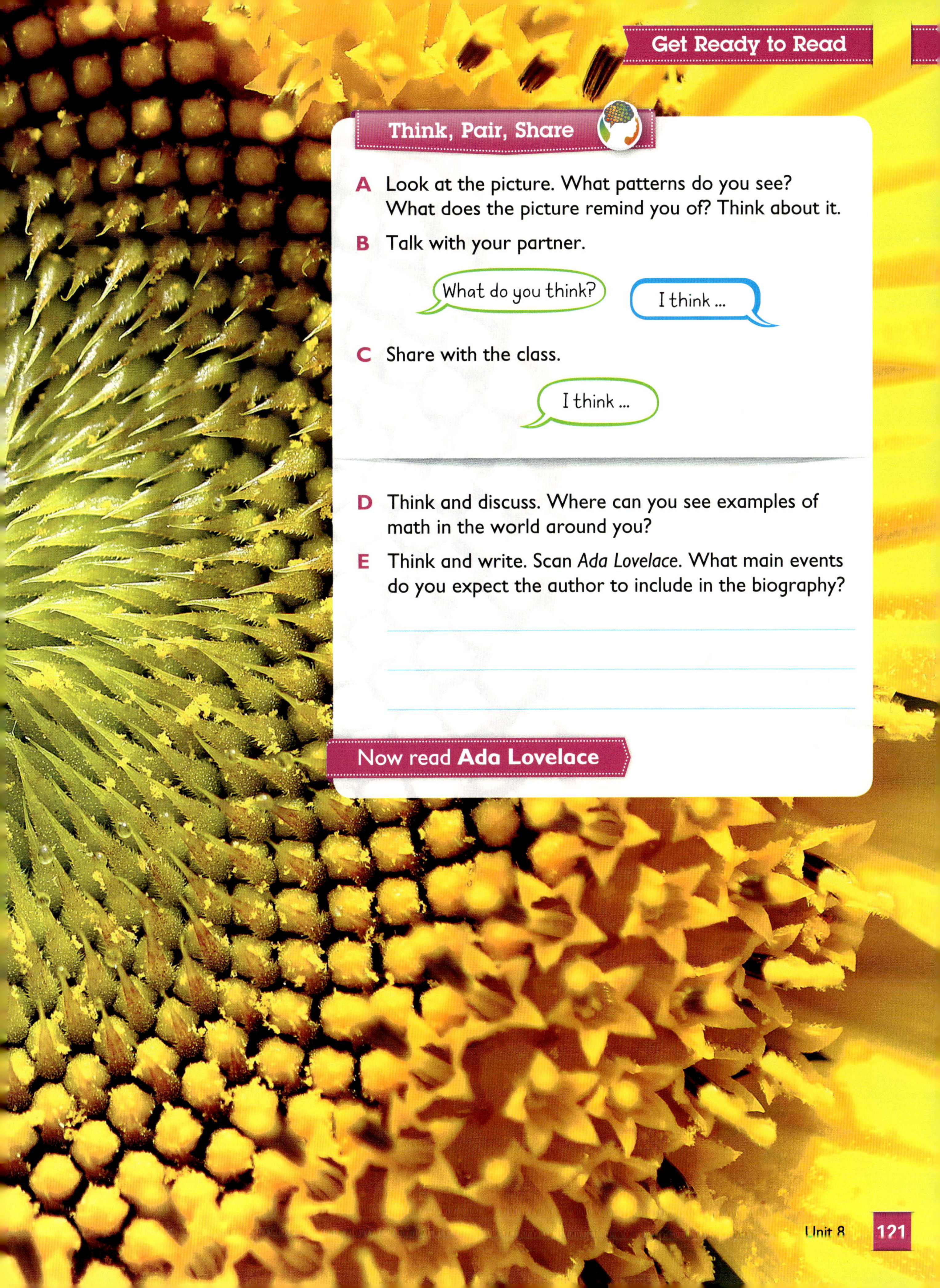

Think, Pair, Share

A Look at the picture. What patterns do you see? What does the picture remind you of? Think about it.

B Talk with your partner.

What do you think?

I think ...

C Share with the class.

I think ...

D Think and discuss. Where can you see examples of math in the world around you?

E Think and write. Scan *Ada Lovelace*. What main events do you expect the author to include in the biography?

Now read **Ada Lovelace**

Nonfiction

ADA LOVELACE

Ada Lovelace (1815–1852), born Augusta Ada Byron, led a remarkable life. She was the daughter of Lord George Gordon Byron, the famous poet, and Lady Anne Isabella Milbanke Byron. Her mother, who had studied math, didn't want Lovelace to develop her father's creativity and imagination, as she thought this would be bad for her character.

But Lovelace was creative, and she had a brilliant mind.

Do you know how to write a computer program?

As a child, she was always trying to invent things. She designed boats and steam-powered flying machines, and was so fascinated by flying that she wrote a book called *Flyology*. But it was her mathematical ability that really took off when she was a teenager.

Charles Babbage was Professor of Mathematics at Cambridge University in the UK. This position has also been held by Isaac Newton and Stephen Hawking.

In those days, some people believed that women's minds were not strong enough to understand complicated math, but Lovelace didn't let what others thought stop her. She questioned everything and was curious about all sorts of developments in science and technology. It was the time of the Industrial Revolution when new, faster ways of making things were being invented, so there was plenty for her to be excited about.

Lovelace was born into a wealthy family in 1815 and, through her education and social life, she met many famous people of that time in England, including author Charles Dickens and scientist Michael Faraday. At the age of 17, Lovelace was introduced to Charles Babbage, the inventor of the Difference Engine—a huge mechanical calculator. This fascinated Lovelace, who thought it was like a thinking machine!

Words in Context

Find these words in the reading. What do you think they mean?

Industrial Revolution **punch cards** **thread** **algebraic** **formulas**

Babbage stopped work on the Difference Engine and started to design a more ambitious machine in 1834—the Analytical Engine. Lovelace asked for the plans to this new machine because she was determined to understand how it worked. She and her mother visited factories to look at different machines. Lovelace noticed how weaving looms and Babbage's engine both used punch cards to operate them. The holes in the cards gave instructions to the machine.

Her way of thinking was, in Lovelace's own words, "poetical science." She believed that creativity and imagination were essential in scientific thinking. Lovelace's creative mind allowed her to see the potential of how technology could be used in the future. Her ideas went beyond making calculations. She imagined technology for making music, creating images, and for other practical purposes. She was ahead of her time. She predicted a digital future.

"The Analytical Engine weaves algebraic patterns, just as the Jacquard loom weaves flowers and leaves."
—Ada Lovelace

Babbage was extremely impressed with Lovelace's mathematical ability and creativity. It was the start of a long friendship and they worked together to develop the Analytical Engine.

In 1842, an Italian mathematician named Luigi Menabrea wrote an article about the Analytical Engine. Lovelace translated the article into English and published it under the name A.A.L., to hide her identity. She added so many of her own detailed notes, formulas, and diagrams that her article was three times longer than the original. These notes contained what many now believe to be the first computer program.

Why do you think Lovelace wanted to hide her identity on her published article?

Unfortunately, the complete Analytical Engine was never built, so Lovelace's program was never tested. She died in 1852, when she was only 36. Her notes have become some of the most important documents in computing history. They were published again 100 years later and inspired many mathematicians working on the first modern computers in the second half of the 20th century. All computer programs today are based on the ideas suggested by Ada Lovelace.

"That brain of mine is something more than merely mortal, as time will show."
—Ada Lovelace

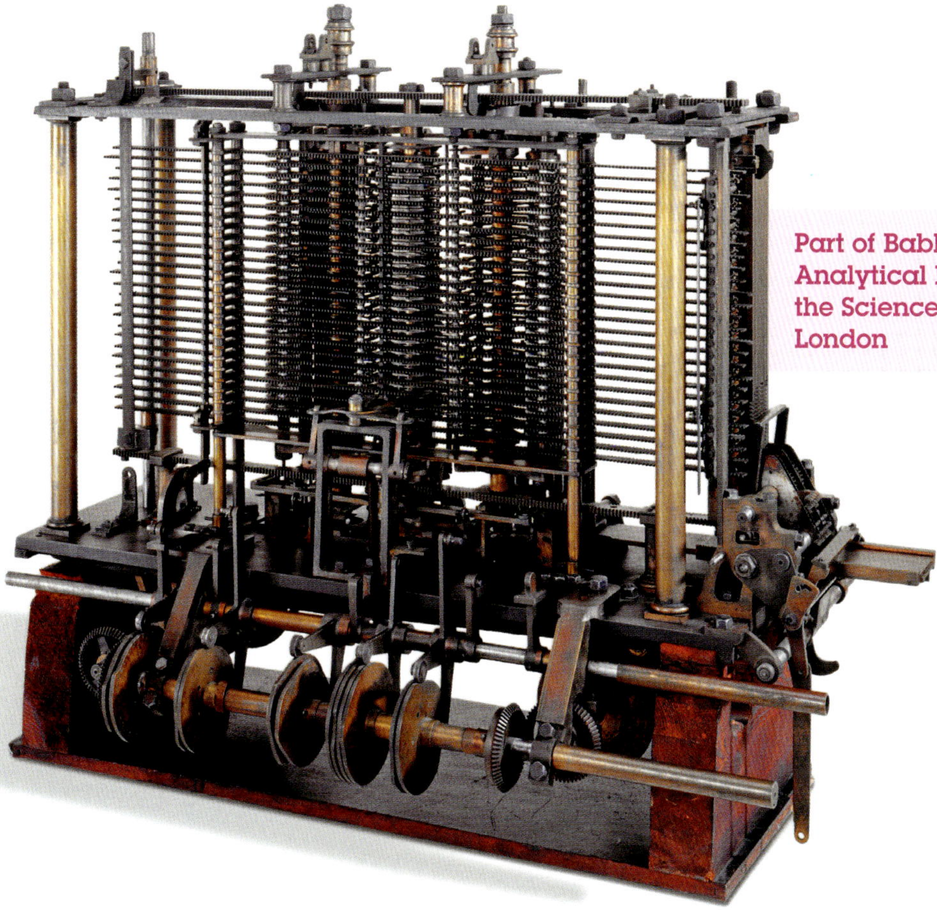

Part of Babbage's Analytical Engine, the Science Museum, London

Since 2009, there has been an Ada Lovelace Day in October, celebrated every year to help inspire women in science, technology, engineering, and math. She has also had a computer programming language named after her, and has been the subject of many books and films, both fact and fiction.

What subject fascinates you?

Explore the Reading

A Answer the questions.

1 Why did Lovelace's mother encourage her mathematical ability?

2 Which of Babbage's inventions was Lovelace first interested in, and what did it do?

3 Which of Babbage's inventions was similar to weaving looms, and in what way?

4 Why did Lovelace call her way of thinking "poetical science"?

5 Why were Lovelace's detailed notes on Luigi Menabrea's article so important?

B Think and write. Find these numbers in the reading. Explain the significance of each number.

Number	Importance
17	
1842	
1815	
36	

C Think and discuss. How might things be different now if Babbage and Lovelace had built the complete Analytical Engine in the 19th century?

Literary Term Open Compound

An **open compound** is a word formed when two unique words are joined together with a space between them to make a new meaning.

Underline the open compounds.

1 There was a full moon in the sky that night.

2 I carried the package into town but the post office was closed.

3 He put the laundry in the washing machine.

4 The water in the hotel's swimming pool was too cold to swim in.

Now find more open compounds in the reading.

A Look back at *The Boy who Drew Cats* in Unit 5. Match the main events of the story to the different stages in the story structure.

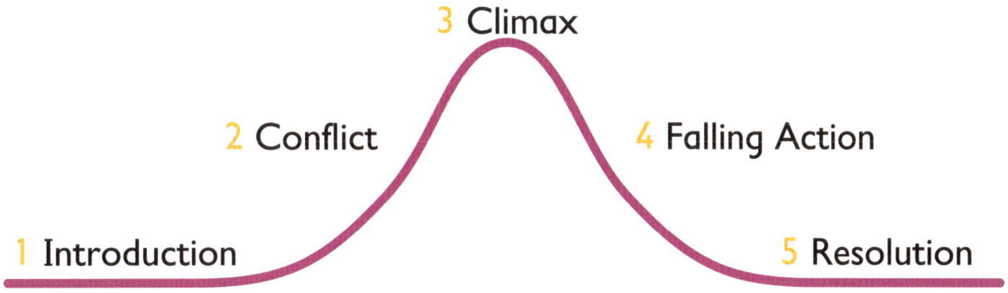

- ☐ Hundreds of rats come to the village.
- ☐ Everyone is pleased that his drawings have saved them from the rats.
- ☐ Jun's parents realize that their son has done something special.
- ☐ Jun loves drawing cats but his parents aren't happy about it.
- ☐ Jun draws so many cats that the rats are terrified and leave the village.

> The best stories have a carefully planned **story structure**. At the beginning, the **introduction** information is given. The setting and characters are introduced. Next, the **conflict**, or problem the characters need to solve, is revealed. In the middle, the plot reaches a high point, or **climax**. Then, the characters work toward solving the problem in the **falling action**. Finally, the story ends with the **resolution** of conflict.

B **Think and discuss. Why is each stage of the story important? What would happen without each stage?**

C **Think and write. Find these sentences and phrases in the reading. Replace the symbols with the mathematical words.**

1 She was quite good at estimating the (%) __________ of cheese and tomato, too.

2 All I wanted was to (÷) __________ my time between playing cello and doing calculations.

3 There are beats and ($\frac{1}{2}$) __________ beats, ($\frac{1}{4}$) __________ and ($\frac{1}{8}$) __________ notes.

4 So this doesn't have to be approached as a (01101) __________ decision?

Now read The Binary Life

The Binary Life

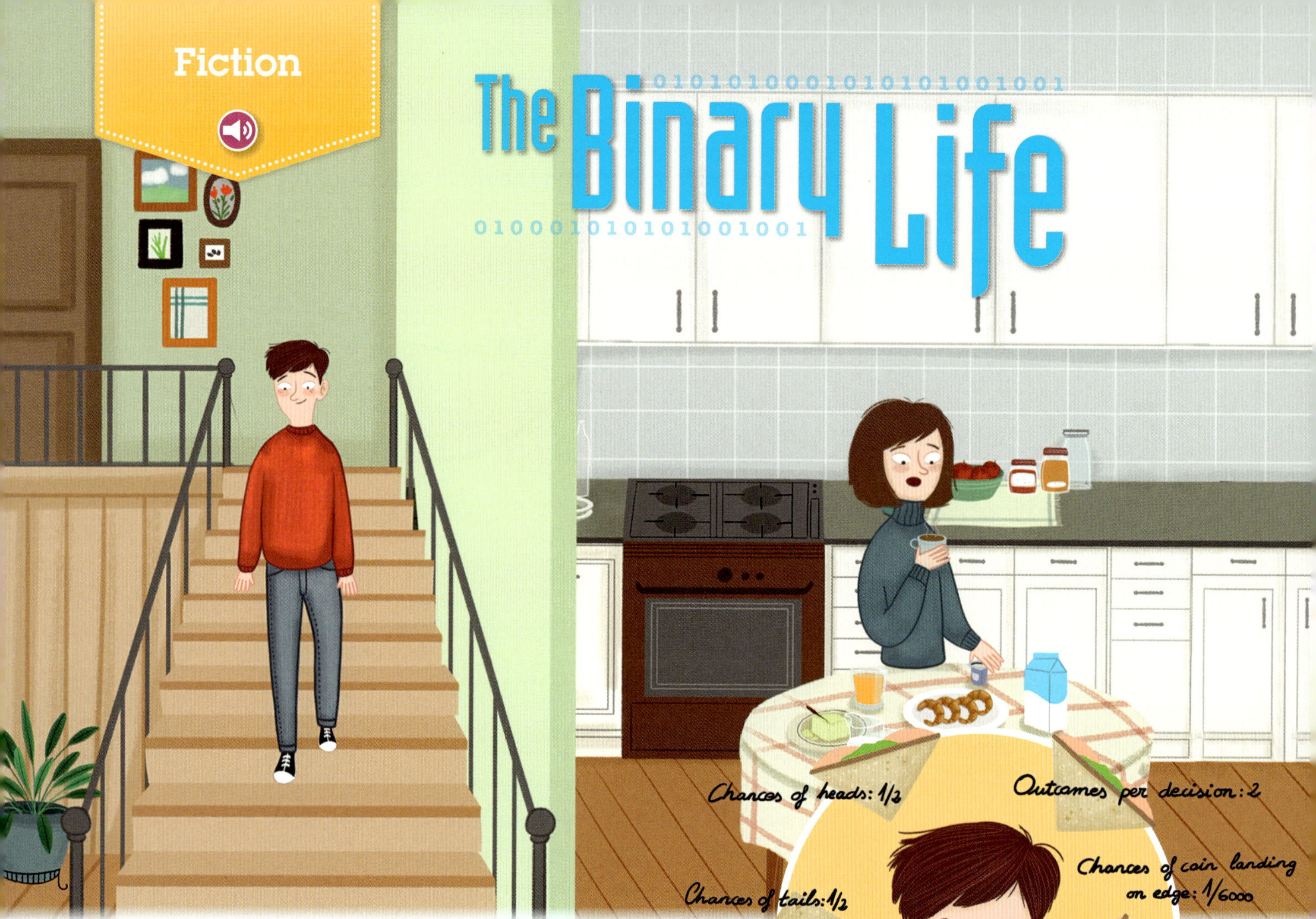

I like to count the steps when I walk downstairs. It makes me feel calm. There are 10 …

"What do you want for breakfast, Dexter?"

The questions start as soon as I get up in the morning.

"Cheese or chicken in your sandwich today? Do you want tomato or lettuce on it? Apple or banana for dessert?"

I don't like all these questions, but I do like the way Mom cut my sandwich into four equal triangles. She's good at estimating the percentage of sandwich toppings, too. I like 75% cheese, 25% tomato.

How do you think someone who is brilliant at math might see the world?

We make an average of 35,000 decisions every day. There are usually way more than two possible outcomes to each decision. But, if there *were* only two possible results, that means there are possibly 2^{35000} ways my day could go. I like to analyze things mathematically. I translate the world into a language I'm comfortable with.

My brain couldn't stop thinking about this, so I had an idea—I could make life easier by flipping a coin to decide everything. Of course, there's a 1 in 6,000 chance of the coin landing on its edge but, if I flip it again, that possibility can be removed from the equation.

A protagonist who doesn't have the expected characteristics of a hero is called an **anti-hero**. He might not be cool, handsome, strong, successful, smart, or kind.

Tails. Green T-shirt.

Heads. Red shorts.

Many of my decisions have been made in this way ...

"What *are* you wearing Dexter? It's freezing!"

This technique doesn't always work well, but at least I don't have to think about it. That frees up my brain to concentrate on music. I play cello, and I like to compose.

It started last autumn …

"You're a natural musician. I'll be disappointed if you don't study music in college," Ms. Park said.

"Math is clearly your subject. You'll go far if you major in math," Mr. Diaz told me.

But I already knew this. That was my problem. This time, problem solving couldn't be done by the flip of a coin and I was getting more and more stressed. All I wanted was to divide my time between playing cello and doing calculations. Why couldn't they see that?

When I'm stressed I think everything can be solved with math, and I believed I could calculate my way out of this confusion. So I started to write—numbers, equations, formulas. But as I wrote, I started to hear music in my head and forgot about the problem completely. The number sequences poured out of my pen. The hours passed and I wrote through the night.

Words in Context

Find these words in the reading. What do you think they mean?

outcome | **free up** | **symmetrical** | **fractions** | **approached**

“No homework? This isn’t like you, Dexter. You don’t have a choice about homework. Homework *must* be done.”

“Sorry, ma’am.”

“What’s wrong, Dexter?”

“I’m not sure, but I spent all night writing music.”

“Really? Wow! Tell me, who’s your favorite composer?”

“Bach.”

“Why?”

“Well, in this piece here the notes go up. Then the same sequence of notes is repeated here, but upside down—it’s symmetrical.”

“And you like symmetry?”

“Yeah. I like all math.”

“So do you think math helps your music?”

“Well, listening to music feels like counting, and when I compose I see numbers, patterns, and waves. Rhythm looks like fractions to me. There are beats and half beats, quarter and eighth notes. You understand what I’m saying, don’t you?”

“Yes, Dexter, I do. You know, there’s a college that teaches computer-based musical composition. I could find the details for you if you want.”

“So this doesn’t have to be approached as a binary decision?”

“Exactly! Don’t think about it like you have to choose.”

“What do you think are the chances of me getting into the program?”

“Oh, about 90%!”

So here I am on my first day at college. I’m nervous, but I have to go now. Class starts in fifteen minutes. I’ve given up on the coin flipping, but I still have all these steps to count. Wish me luck!

Explore the Reading

A How does Dexter use numbers and math in the story? Match the two sentence halves.

1 He likes three-quarters cheese …
2 He flips a coin …
3 He counts the stairs …
4 When he's stressed …
5 When he listens to Bach …
6 When he composes …

a. he writes numbers.
b. he notices symmetry.
c. and one quarter tomato.
d. to help him make decisions.
e. to make him feel calm.
f. he sees patterns and waves.

B Think, write, and discuss. Which of Dexter's decisions do you think are binary? Why? What binary decisions have you made?

C Imagine what happens to Dexter after *The Binary Life*. Write the story structure for the next chapter.

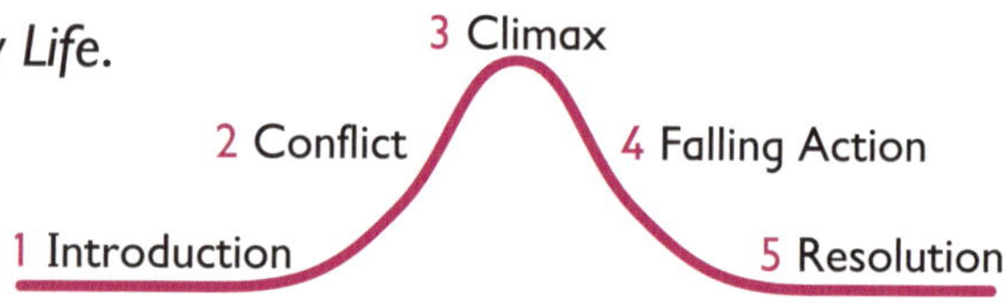

1

2

3

4

5

D Think and write. What do you do when you have a difficult choice to make? Why?

Why are numbers important in our lives?

A Compare and contrast Ada from *Ada Lovelace* and Dexter from *The Binary Life*. Complete the Venn diagram.

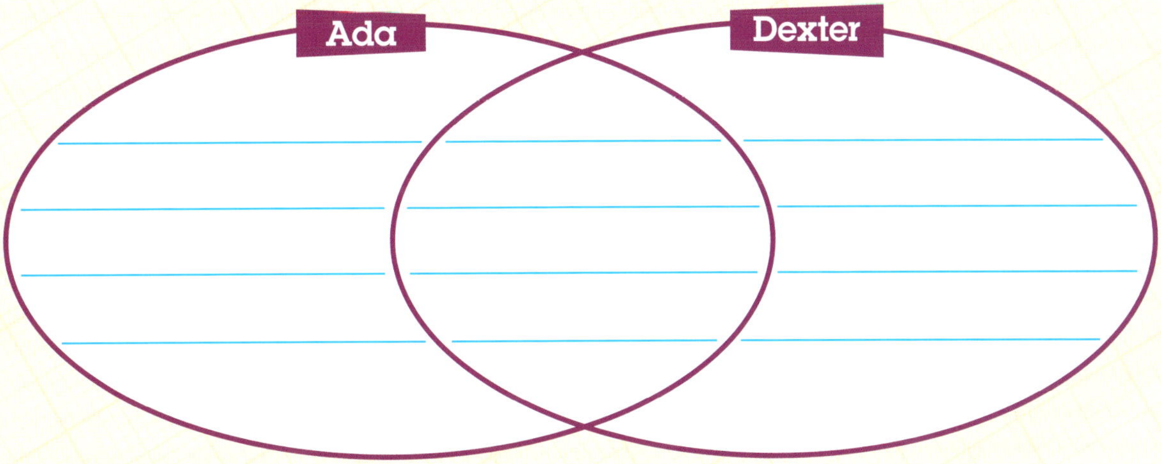

B What are some ways you use numbers in your daily life? Do an Inside Outside Circle.

C Think and write. Do you prefer numbers or words, or do you prefer both? How does that have an effect on your daily life?

My Reading Journal

Do you think any of the characters from the readings are remarkable? Why?

Did this unit make you think differently about math? Why or why not?

Go back to page 121. **What new thoughts do you have to share?**

UNIT 9

Make Up Your Mind

Step Inside

A Look at the picture. Choose a person or a thing. What can they see?

Let's choose the boy with his mother ...

He can see ...

B What do you think they believe?

I think he believes ...

Maybe ...

C What do you think they care about?

I think he cares about ...

Yes, and ...

D Think and discuss. What is a decision? What decisions do we make every day?

E Think and predict. Then write. Look at the picture from *Making Decisions*. What do you think the girl is feeling? Why might she be feeling that way?

Now read **Making Decisions**

Nonfiction

Making Decisions

How do you make decisions?

Lena is a good volleyball player. Her serve is excellent, and she is good at passing. But Lena doesn't get much game time. The rest of the girls on the A team are so strong, Lena spends more time watching on the bench than playing.

After volleyball practice, Coach Williams calls Lena over for a chat. The coach offers Lena a choice. This season, she can drop down to the B team, where she'll play every game and be one of their better players, or she can stick with the A team. The decision is hers.

What should any of us do when we're faced with making an important decision? What should our strategy be?

Stop and Think!

We want an answer right now. We feel the pressure to decide quickly. But rushing into a decision doesn't allow us time to consider it properly. Next time you have an important decision to make, stop and think first.

Big or Small?

Not every decision is important. What you're going to eat for lunch is a small choice. Which school you go to is a big one. Learn to recognize which decisions are big and need careful thought, and which ones you shouldn't worry about too much.

It's Good to Talk

Ask a friend or adult for advice. They may have a new and different way of looking at the problem.

Cut Down Your Choices

Sometimes, having too many choices makes it a struggle to come to a decision. From a list of options, you can remove the ones that don't help you meet the goal or can't be done. This will give you fewer things to pick from.

Pros and Cons List

One technique to help make a decision is to make a **Pros and Cons List**. Look at your options. For each one, write down all the reasons it's a good choice: the pros. Next, make a list of all the negatives: the cons. A list like this can show you which choice is the one with the most pros and the smallest number of cons.

Homework	
Pros	Cons
Learning Good grades Responsibility	Work

Movie	
Pros	Cons
Fun	No time to do homework Learning? Bad grades?

Words in Context

Find these words in the reading. What do you think they mean?

on the bench | stick with | pressure | cut down | human nature

Steps to Making Decisions

1 Define the problem or decision.

Stop and think about what the problem is. Then consider whether it's a big or small problem.

2 Make a list of your options.

Research and brainstorm the options to solve the problem. You might also ask someone for advice.

3 Evaluate your ideas.

Look at the ideas that you came up with. Cut down your options.

4 Consider the consequences.

From the options still available, think about what the results might be for each one. Make a pros and cons list.

5 Decide on a solution.

Review all of the information you have and decide which option you feel best about. Then take action.

6 Reflect on the results of the decision.

Think about what happened after you made the decision. Were you happy with the results?

Sometimes we make the wrong decision, but it's part of human nature. It happens to everyone. What is important is to reflect on why we got it wrong, and learn for the future. We need to recognize that if we had made a different decision, the outcome might have been better.

Common reasons for making poor decisions are:

Pressure from our friends is called **peer pressure**. Peer means someone who is the same age as you or is in an equal position as you.

Lena's Decision

To make a careful decision, Lena follows the steps.

1 Define the problem or decision.

Lena tells her coach she needs some time to think. She goes home and sits alone. *Which volleyball team should I play for this season?*

2 Make a list of your options.

I could play for the A team, drop down to the B team, or quit playing volleyball.

3 Evaluate your ideas.

I like volleyball a lot and don't want to quit, so I'll eliminate that option.

Playing for A Team	
Pros	**Cons**
• A team is a better team. • I'll have to push myself really hard.	• I'll hardly ever get to play in competitive games. • I'll have to push myself really hard.

Playing for B Team	
Pros	**Cons**
• I'll get lots of game time. • I can be the leader of this team. • Having a chance to lead a team is important to me.	• B Team isn't as good as A Team.

When was the last time you had to make a decision in a hurry? What did you decide?

4 Consider the consequences.

Lena makes a pros and cons list to help her look at possible outcomes.

5 Decide on a solution.

I'll play for the B team and then try for the A team again next season.

6 Reflect on the results of the decision.

I think I got a lot stronger playing so much and it made me a better player.

Whichever strategy you choose, it's important to have a range of strategies in your decision-making toolbox, ready to pull out when you need them most. And remember, every mistake is an opportunity to learn and grow!

Explore the Reading

A Think and write. Choose the strategy that matches each sentence.

It's Good to Talk **Stop and Think!** **Cut Down Your Choices** **Big or Small?** **Pros and Cons List**

1 Learn to recognize which decisions are big and need careful thought, and which ones you shouldn't worry about too much. ____________

2 Having too many choices makes it a struggle to come to a decision. ____________

3 Ask a friend or adult for advice. ____________

4 Look at your options. For each one, write down all the things that make it a good choice. Next, make a list of all the negatives. ____________

5 Next time you have an important decision to make, stop and think first. ____________

B Think and write. Imagine you have a difficult decision with two choices. A friend says you should just flip a coin. Is that a good strategy? Why or why not?

____

C Think, discuss, and write. Do you agree with Lena's decision? What would you have done in her position?

____

D Think and discuss. What do each of these people think about in each situation?

1 A student with a big test next week.

2 A teacher assigning homework.

3 A world leader making difficult decisions.

A Read, think, and write. List two of the conflicts Pia faces in *Urgent Message*. Describe these conflicts.

Pia looked at her laptop screen. There was the message. But no username or personal information. This was weird. She'd never seen a message without a username before. Pia got up and showed her parents.

"It's a trick," said Dad with a yawn. "Soon they'll ask you for money."

"Never reply to strange messages, you know better than that," said Mom.

"OK," agreed Pia. But she couldn't help feeling a little anxious.

The second message arrived later that day while Pia was playing a video game online.

No name, no ID. The message gave Pia the heebie-jeebies.

"-oat s-nk"? Pia didn't understand. *Goat stink*? *Float sank*?

____

____

External conflict in a story is when there is a difference between characters or ideas, such as a disagreement, an argument, or even a fight.

When a character in a story has an **internal conflict**, they are facing a difficult personal choice, or are having trouble making a decision.

B Read and write. Are these conflicts external (*E*) or internal (*I*)?

1 "Should I go out with my friends or help my brother? I just don't know." ____

2 Max arrives early to be the first in line, but Edward cuts the line. ____

3 Someone says, "Your picture looks ridiculous!" ____

4 Sara finds a phone in the street. Should she hand it in, or keep it for herself? ____

C Think and write. Look at the first picture from *It's Not OK*. Do you think the girl is facing an internal or external conflict? Why?

D Think and discuss. Think of a time when you faced a tough decision. What happened?

Now read **It's Not OK**

Fiction

It's Not OK

Why are some decisions hard to make?

While Miral waited for the school bus, her phone beeped: it was a message notification from Dana. Miral opened the app.

The photo stayed on Miral's screen for a moment, then the app made it vanish, as if it had never been there at all. But Miral had seen it. Penny would have seen it, too. It was Penny with the new braces on her teeth. People could be so mean sometimes.

Miral shoved her phone into the pocket of her backpack, trying to pretend the photo had never existed.

In school, Miral saw Penny. Miral forced a weak smile. “What’s up?” she asked.

Penny shrugged. “Not much.”

Miral saw the phone in Penny’s hands, her fingers wrapped tightly around it. She thought of the photo. *What should I say?* “Did you do your homework?” asked Miral, filling the deafening silence.

“Uh-huh,” said Penny.

“Tough, wasn’t it?”

“Uh-huh.”

Who is the **antagonist** (the character or situation the protagonist must overcome) in this story?

Penny didn’t say much at school that day. Miral didn’t say much either.

Words in Context

Find these words in the reading. What do you think they mean?

notification **shoved** **deafening silence** **guts** **selfies**

It didn't stop there.

Over the next few days, there was a photo of a grinning donkey saying "Hee-haw." A photo of train tracks. A photo of Penny with a funny smile.

Each time, Miral burned inside.

"How funny was that donkey?" said James at lunch.

Miral shook her head. She looked around the room. Penny was sitting by herself.

Maybe Penny doesn't care about the jokes, thought Miral. *Dana will get bored with teasing soon, right? It'll become old news, and we can forget it ever happened. It'll go away, right?*

Miral gave Penny an embarrassed wave. Penny waved back.

"Hee-haw," laughed James as he left.

Miral felt cold as she finished her lunch. If she'd had the guts, she would have told James to be quiet and leave Penny alone.

Later that week, Penny wasn't at badminton. She was always at badminton. Miral helped the other kids set up the nets while Dana took selfies with her friends.

Miral's phone beeped. It was Dana's photo. "Badminton Club! EVERYONE'S here."

Not everyone, Miral thought. *I should do something about this.* She sighed and put her phone away.

That night, Miral got another message. Someone had saved the donkey message and was sharing it again. Before the photo had a chance to vanish, Miral quickly copied it onto her phone. The phone felt hot in her hands. *Now what?*

She did nothing, set her phone on her desk, and tried to get to sleep. *But if the photo had been of me, what would I have done?* Miral wondered.

The next morning, Miral made a decision. Before school started, she went to the assistant principal's office and knocked on the door.

"I need to show you something, Mr. Costa," she said. Miral opened up her phone, her hands shaking. "It's making fun of Penny—she just got new braces," she explained.

Miral watched as the smile dropped from Mr. Costa's face. Miral swallowed.

"It's been going on for a while," she admitted. "It's kind of an open secret."

"Would you like to tell me why you're only telling me now?" asked Mr. Costa gently. Miral went red. She looked down at the floor. "Sometimes it's hard to know what to do, isn't it?" said Mr. Costa.

Miral nodded.

"Leave it with me," said Mr. Costa. "You've spoken out now. Off you go to class."

In class, Miral sat down beside Penny. “You weren’t at badminton yesterday,” said Miral.

Penny shrugged. “Didn’t feel like going.”

“About those photos,” said Miral quickly. “I think they’re really mean. Your braces look fine. If I’d been brave, I would have said something before. I’m sorry.”

“That’s OK,” said Penny.

“No, it’s not. It’s really not,” said Miral. As she spoke, she gave Dana a long stare. Dana went bright red.

“Friends?” Miral asked hopefully.

“Friends,” replied Penny.

“Badminton after school?” asked Miral.

“Sounds good,” said Penny with a big, beautiful smile.

Who would you talk to if you or someone you knew was being bullied?

Explore the Reading

A Complete the story mountain with the main events from *It's Not OK*.

3 Climax

2 Conflict

4 Falling action

1 Introduction

Main characters:

Main setting:

5 Resolution

B Think and write. What internal conflict do you think Dana might be having at the end of the story?

C Think and discuss. Why do you think going to see Mr. Costa was such a difficult choice for Miral to make?

D Think and discuss. What do you think might have happened if Miral had decided to take action about the bullying when it started?

Literary Term Oxymoron

An **oxymoron** is an expression that contains words with opposite meanings.

Underline the oxymorons.

1 She was clearly confused by the explanation.

2 Going back home was a bittersweet experience.

3 I've just read a seriously funny book.

4 Theirs was a love/hate relationship.

Now find three pairs of oxymorons in the reading.

How do we handle difficult choices?

A Think and write. How could Miral from *It's Not OK* have used Lena's six steps from *Making Decisions* to decide what to do?

1 Define the decision or problem. What decision is Miral trying to make?

2 Make a list of her options.

3 Evaluate the ideas. What information does she have?

4 Consider the consequences.

5 Decide on a solution.

6 Reflect on the results of the decision.

B Make a list. What kinds of decisions do you have to make in your life? Think of an example for each kind. Do a Think, Pair, Share.

C Choose one of the decisions from your list in **B**. Choose a decision-making strategy and make a decision. What might the consequences of your decision be?

My Reading Journal

Has this unit helped you in any way? Why or why not?

Write a review of the unit.

Go back to page 137. **Do the routine again.**

UNIT 10 Take the Lead

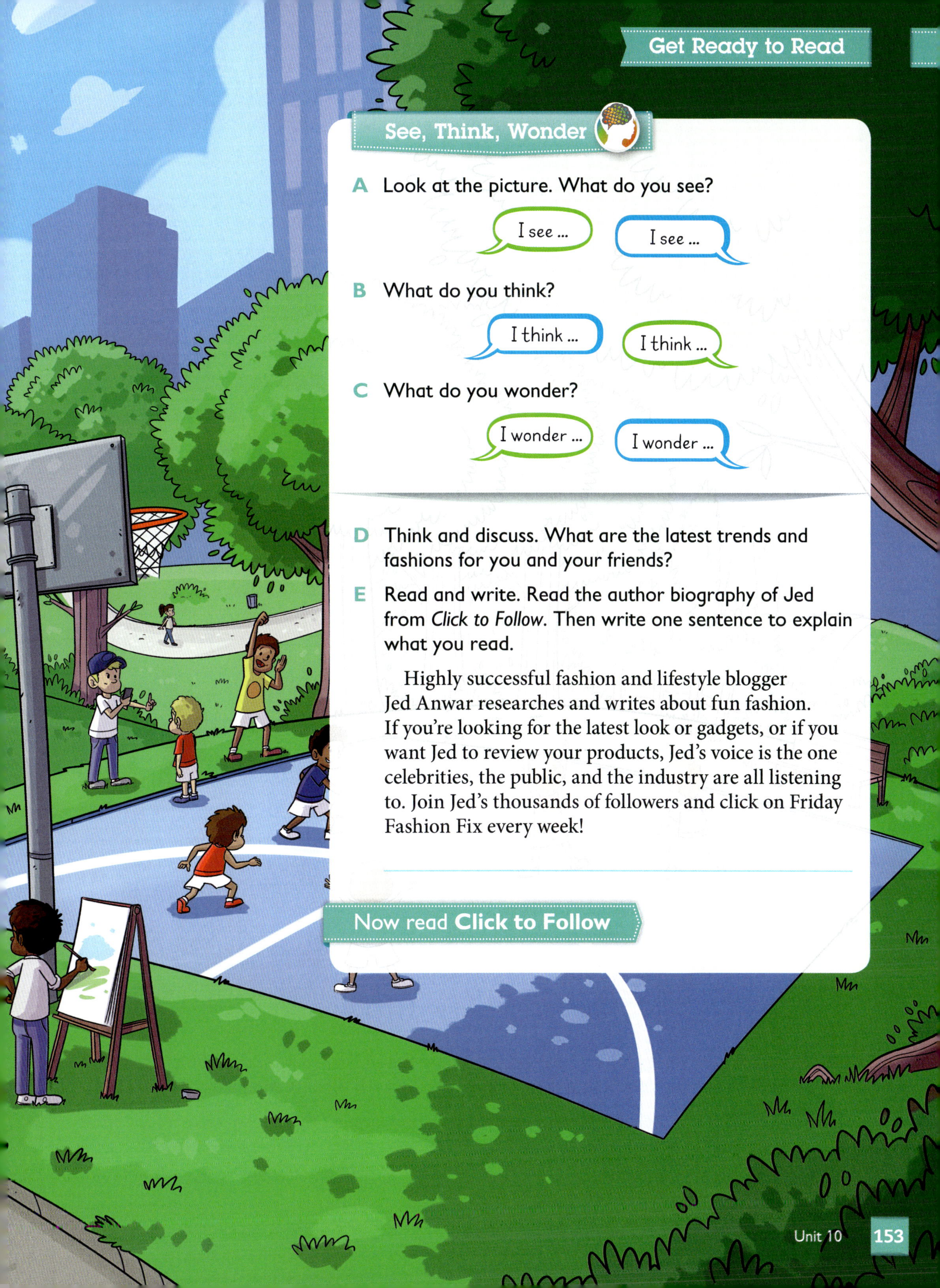

See, Think, Wonder

A Look at the picture. What do you see?

I see ... I see ...

B What do you think?

I think ... I think ...

C What do you wonder?

I wonder ... I wonder ...

D Think and discuss. What are the latest trends and fashions for you and your friends?

E Read and write. Read the author biography of Jed from *Click to Follow*. Then write one sentence to explain what you read.

Highly successful fashion and lifestyle blogger Jed Anwar researches and writes about fun fashion. If you're looking for the latest look or gadgets, or if you want Jed to review your products, Jed's voice is the one celebrities, the public, and the industry are all listening to. Join Jed's thousands of followers and click on Friday Fashion Fix every week!

Now read **Click to Follow**

Fiction

Click to Follow

Scene 1: Inside a bright office

(*Jed looks through magazines. Lucie is typing on her laptop.*)

Jed: I need something new for this week's Friday Fashion Fix blog post.

Lucie: (*types*) Just write the same as you always do, Jed—what you're wearing, what celebrities are wearing, what your readers should be wearing, upload a photo, done!

Jed: Does it really sound that formulaic?

Lucie: It's the same with my food blog. Where to eat, what to eat, photo, post! People love it! What's wrong?

Jed: Well, writing about clothes was always my dream, but it's not the same as it used to be.

(*Lucie walks over to Jed.*)

Lucie: You tell people what's hot and what's not! Those Speed Feet sneakers you blogged about last month—everyone wants them. People buy what you tell them is cool. Isn't that great?

Jed: No, it isn't! If I told people to wear an actual watermelon on their head, chances are some of them would do it!

Lucie: So?

Do you write or follow a blog?

Jed: (*sighs*) I'm known for my blog style, and I've become connected with the brands I write about.

Lucie: I know. I think it's so cool that companies send you products to review.

Jed: (*holds up each item*) Look what came today—aluminum shorts, shoes that look like duck feet, glasses without any glass in them!

Lucie: People love crazy fashion. It's all about clicks, likes, and follows, right? And you have thousands of followers. You add fun to people's lives.

Jed: But I'm not having fun. I'm not excited anymore.

Lucie: So make some fun! Give your readers some interesting styles to try.

Jed: Yeah, maybe you're right, this calls for a photo shoot. Danny!

Danny: (*pulls out a camera*) On it, Jed!

Lucie: Perfect! Let's livestream it.

Words in Context

Find these words in the reading. What do you think they mean?

formulaic   take me seriously   ethically   authentic   influential

A play typically consists of a series of **scenes**. A new scene starts when the time or place changes.

Scene 2: The photo shoot

(*Tamara wearing different strange fashion items. Danny is taking pictures. Jed is looking at the laptop.*)

Jed: Amazing! People are loving it!

Tamara: (*wearing a pair of shorts over her pants*) How about this? The superhero look—shorts on the outside!

Lucie: I like it!

Jed: (*typing*) … We're all superheroes inside, show us your superhero style.

Scene 3: Jed's living room

(*Jed is sitting at home working on his next blog.*)

Reporter 1: (*on television*) … a clothing factory collapsed today injuring 16 workers …

Jed: That's awful. (*changes the channel*)

Reporter 2: (*on television*) … A chemical leak at the Speed Feet sneaker factory has polluted the local water supply.

Jed: Why do things like this happen so often? I wonder … (*searches on his laptop*) There's so much I didn't know about this … Someone should really say something to raise awareness. (*Jed thinks.*) I have an idea! But will people take me seriously?

Scene 4: In the office

Lucie: (*reading*) "StyleGuru says that next season we'll be wearing yellow. But I'll be wearing green. That means I'll only buy clothes that are ethically produced. Today, I'm going to review a brand that creates clothes that are stylish, affordable, and sustainable …"

Danny: (*reading a response*) "Is somebody else writing this blog now?"

Jed: I'm losing my audience.

Lucie: Maybe it's not the right audience for you anymore.

Jed: I think I'm OK with that. Before, I just wanted them to like me. Now it feels better to write about something important.

Danny: Hey, look at this comment! (*reads*) "We all love cool clothes and gadgets. But let's think about where our things have come from and where they're going …"

Tamara: Here's another one! (*reads*) "I love this! Wanna start a clothes swap campaign with us?"

Jed: Guys, I just got an email from Green Threads. They make sustainable clothes and they want to have a meeting with me.

What do you think *Wanna* is short for?

Scene 5: The office, the next day

Reporter 1: (*on the laptop*) The makers of Speed Feet sneakers announced a plan to review how their products are made.

Jed: I can't believe I used to promote those sneakers.

Lucie: Your message is so much more authentic, this sounds like the real you. You seem much happier and motivated now.

Tamara: Yeah, and you were invited to attend Fashion Week to report on ethical fashion. They actually called you one of the most influential young voices in fashion.

Jed: (*sits back*) Yup, I think I've found my voice, and it feels great to use it to set a good example.

Explore the Reading

A Read, think, and write. What is inferred by these statements? Write the meaning.

1 Well, writing about clothes was always my dream, but it's not the same as it used to be.

______

2 If I told people to wear an actual watermelon on their head, chances are some of them would do it!

______

3 It's all about clicks, likes, and follows, right?

______

4 I'll be wearing green.

______

5 Yup, I think I've found my voice, and it feels great to use it to set a good example.

______

B Think, write, and discuss. Describe Jed's character and write the evidence for each description.

creative ______ ______

______ ______

______ ______

C Think and discuss. What should you think about before you click to follow a blog?

Literary Term Assonance

Assonance is the repetition of the same sound inside words that are next to each other or close together.

Listen. Then underline the assonance. Then write three more sentences or phrases using assonance.

1 You don't have to have the latest, greatest clothes to look good.

2 Kniffen has the top job in the company.

3 This store sells cool shoes.

4 ______

5 ______

6 ______

Now find more examples of assonance in the reading.

A Complete the table. Read the main ideas from *Click to Follow*. Look back at the play. Find at least one important supporting detail for each main idea.

Main Ideas	Supporting Details
Jed doesn't feel inspired by his work.	
He tries to make his work more fun.	
He hears bad news about the conditions in clothing factories.	
He decides to write about more important things.	

Summarizing helps us to focus on the main ideas and the important details that support them in a reading, without being distracted by minor details. Summarizing helps us pick out the main ideas and to remember what we've read.

B Read, think, and write. Complete the table.

Fashion can be fun! Wearing a red coat can give us confidence. Clothes made for fashion shows are different than clothes sold in stores. They are fitted to each model to show off the designs, but models are often tall and thin. Many people in the real world will never look like models in the same clothes, though they dream of looking like them. This can have a negative effect on young people and ruin the positive power of fashion.

Main Idea	Important Supporting Details	Minor Details/ Unimportant Examples

C Read and write. Read the first paragraph of *Recycle Runway*. Write one sentence to summarize the paragraph.

D Think and discuss. Look at the pictures from *Recycle Runway*. What do you think Nancy Judd's job is? Why?

Now read **Recycle Runway**

Nonfiction

Recycle Runway

HANDMADE BY NANCY JUDD

People have been fascinated by clothes and influenced by fashion for as long as we've had mirrors. Clothes offer us a way to be the same as everyone else, or a way to express our individuality. But what if they could do much more than that? What if beautiful clothes could help us deliver a more important message?

How do you think fashion affects the environment?

Nancy Judd creates fashion sculptures from trash. But her purpose isn't just to show us her wonderful designs, it's to teach us about the environment—Judd is an artist and a passionate environmental educator. She is committed to getting people to look differently at waste and to change the way they live on Earth. The Aluminum Drop Dress Judd is wearing in the photo is made from an old shower curtain covered with drop-shaped metal pieces cut out from soda cans. Recycling cans reduces the use of natural resources and chemicals.

"What if beautiful clothes could help deliver a more important message?"

Judd started the Recycle Runway project while working as the Recycling Coordinator for the City of Santa Fe in New Mexico, USA. She realized that art and fashion could be a fun and positive way to deliver her message, so she organized a recycled fashion contest. To promote this event, Judd created some upcycled outfits, and this gave her the idea for a special collection of designs.

Exhibitions of these sustainable fashion designs are shown in airports, museums, and shopping malls. The clothes have received worldwide media attention, generating interest from big companies to sponsor her work.

ReDress Upcycled Style is the name of Judd's traveling museum exhibition of 18 outfits, pictured here at Bascom: A Center for the Visual Arts.

Why do you think the designs are displayed in airports, museums, and shopping malls?

Judd runs creative workshops for children and adults, and gives presentations about environmental issues. Many of these outfits are made during public workshop events, so people can take part in creating them. The sculptures are inspiring people all over the world to help care for the planet.

Through her amazing creations, Nancy Judd is showing the world that you don't have to be a dedicated follower of fashion. You can make fashion work for you! Maybe in the future we'll all be wearing sustainable clothing, recycling more, and creating less waste.

Words in Context

Find these words in the reading. What do you think they mean?

individuality aluminum upcycled outfits commissioned

The Jellyfish Dress is made of blue, green, and white plastic bags and brings attention to issues about marine conservation. It was created to be displayed in public in a coastal city.

Plastics can seriously harm marine life. Turtles sometimes eat plastic bags, mistaking them for jellyfish, one of their favorite foods. Sea trash such as plastic bottles, plastic bags, and cans are all recyclable.

Tireless Couture is made from the inside of car and bicycle tires. It was commissioned for a city that wanted to encourage people to drive less and use the new pedestrian and cycle paths more. They paid Judd to create this sculpture so that, when people see it, they'll remember to use the car less and bicycle more to reduce their carbon footprint.

More than 1 billion car tires are trashed each year.

Faux Fur Coat uses many meters of old video and audiotape, sewn onto a second-hand coat.

Electronic waste often contains glass and valuable metals as well as dangerous chemicals. These materials can be recycled and reused, but the chemicals can get into the soil if electronic waste is thrown away as landfill trash.

Sol Man is a project inspired by 6th grade students that combines art with science to teach about energy conservation. In science they learned about how energy is created and the problems with different energy sources. Then in art they drew their ideas of a superhero character. Judd used their ideas to design the costume for the superhero. The students then helped make the pieces that look like solar panels in their consumer sciences class. They designed and made a new recycled costume called Sol Man. This sculpture is made from trash from energy-efficient building projects. Through this project, the students learned how to save money and energy in their homes.

Have you ever created something new with recycled materials?

Judd encourages us all to make eco-pledges. These are promises to help the environment. We make simple decisions all the time that affect the planet.

What eco-pledges can you make?

Explore the Reading

A **Answer the questions. Find the evidence for each answer. Write the page where you found the answer.**

1 What three things can clothes offer us? ______

______

______

2 What are three reasons why Nancy Judd creates fashion sculptures from trash? ______

______

______

3 What are two ways she showed her designs? ______

______

4 Why do big companies want to sponsor this project? ______

______

B **Think and write. Which sentences express important details (*I*) that can be used to give a summary of the reading? Which ones express minor details (*M*)?**

1 Clothes can deliver important messages. ______

2 Nancy Judd wants to teach us about the environment using her wonderful designs. ______

3 The Aluminum Drop Dress is made from an old shower curtain. ______

4 She shows upcycled outfits at exhibitions in public places. ______

5 She used a second-hand coat to make the Faux Fur Coat. ______

6 The bags used to make the Jellyfish Dress are blue, green, and white. ______

C **Complete the table with details about the fashion sculptures.**

What's it Called?	What's it Made Of?	What's the Message?

D **Think and discuss. What is the difference between recycling and upcycling?**

How are we influenced by things around us?

A Compare and contrast *Click to Follow* and *Recycle Runway*. Complete the Venn diagram.

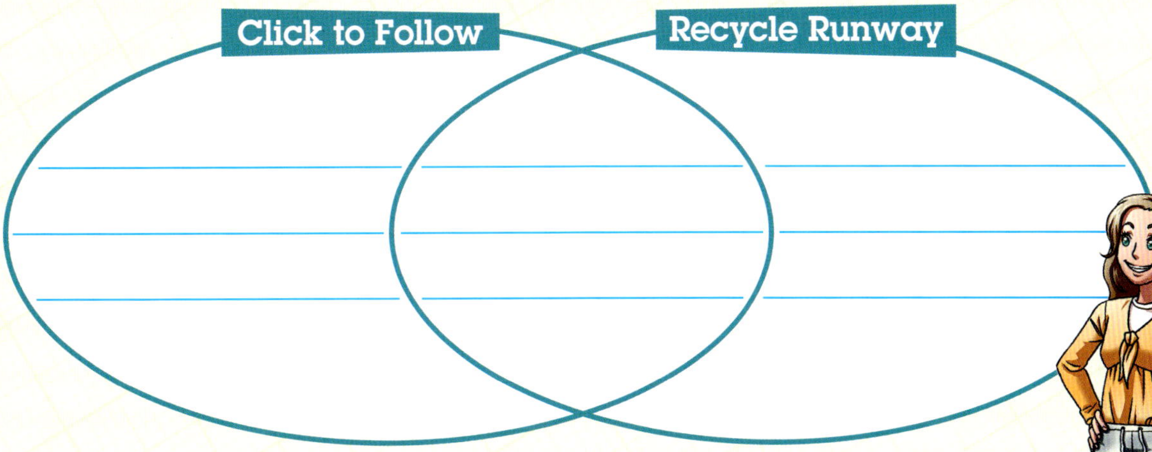

B Who or what influences what you buy, how you think, and what you do? Do a Rally Robin. Make a list.

C Look at the list in **B**. What are the most positive influences in your life? Are there any negative influences?

My Reading Journal

Imagine you are Nancy Judd. Sketch a design for a fashion sculpture and present it to the class.

How did the readings in this book influence you? Is there anything you will change or do in your life as a result of reading them?

Go back to page 153. **What new things do you see, think, or wonder?**

Macmillan Education
4 Crinan Street
London N1 9XW
A division of Springer Nature Limited

Companies and representatives throughout the world

Level 6 Literacy Book ISBN: 978-1-786-32595-2
Level 6 Student Book Pack ISBN: 978-1-380-00269-3

Written by Paul Mason, Viv Lambert, and Mo Choy

First published 2019

Designed by Pronk Media, Inc.

Illustrated by Adam Horsepool (Advocate Art) pp. 4, 6; Emiliano Ordás pp. 8–9, 96–103; Szilvia Szakáll (Beehive Illustration) pp. 10–17, 122–127; David Smith (Beehive Illustration) pp. 18–21; Alan Brown (Advocate Art) pp. 26–32; Alexandre Affonso (Advocate Art) pp. 34–39; Chuck Whelon (Beehive Illustration) pp. 42–46; Davide Ortu (Beehive Illustration) pp. 50–54; Maurizio DeAngelis & Pablo Gallego (Beehive Illustration) pp. 59, 61; Ben Barter (Beehive Illustration) pp. 64–70, 152–153; Roger Stewart (Beehive Illustration) pp. 74–78; Juan Manuel Moreno (MB Artists) pp. 80–86; Juanma García Escobar pp. 104–105; Janos Jantner (Beehive Illustration) pp. 106–111; Victor Mclindon (Advocate Art) pp. 114, 116, 118; Beatriz Castro (Advocate Art) pp. 130–135; Carl Morris (Beehive Illustration) pp. 136–142; Gustavo Mazali & Tamara Joubert (Beehive Illustration) pp. 144–149; Leo Campos (Beehive Illustration) pp. 154–160.

Front cover design and concept by 3CD
Cover adaptation by Roberto Martinez
Cover illustration by Juan Manuel Moreno
Cover photograph by Getty Images/Leonello Calvetti/Stocktrek Images (globe)
Picture research by Emily Taylor

Authors' acknowledgements
Paul Mason:
I would like to acknowledge and thank the team at Macmillan Education and RedNova Learning. Working together was a privilege.

Viv Lambert and Mo Choy:
Thanks to Macmillan Education and RedNova Learning for giving us the opportunity to write together again, and for the support and dedication throughout the process from both sides of the pond.

The publishers would like to thank: Colegio Buckingham and Gabriela Rodriguez, Colegio Euterpe and Angélica Sánchez, Colegio Heroes Mexicanos and Marcelo Carlos Hernández Morales, Internaciones Campus Fraijanes and Ana Monica Thomas, New Victoria International College and Ghada Hassan Mokbel, The Southern Cross School and Dayana Acevedo, Antonia Lira, and Paula Jorquera, Verbo Quetzaltenango and Cindy Steicy Ixchiu Velásquez, Salwa Abid, Riham Almughrabi, Maria Pia Ayala, Meryem Bennis, Leticia Blazquez, Angel Bonilla, Victor Cojulun, John Cruft, Silvia Díez de Rivera, Randa Farouk, Magda Giornazi, Vangelina Hernandez, Quyen Ho, Ziad Jadallah, Youngkwang Jang, Faisal M'reish, Jackie Mustoe, Adriana Ochoa, Devrim Ozdemir, Silvia Raya, Ola Refaat, Helen Sharbain, Sana Sifri, Esra Tosun, Lemmy Trujillo, Tamer Victor, Jake Whiddon, Sandra Wu, Amanda Zhang.

The authors and publishers would like to thank the following for permission to reproduce their photographs: **Alamy**/A Astes p. 164(inner tube), Alamy/James Boardman p. 92(tr), Alamy/Heritage Image Partnership Ltd p. 90(bl), Alamy/Richard Heyes p. 92(bl), Alamy/icpix_lab p. 91(tl), Alamy/Steve Lyne p. 90(tr), Alamy/Riccardo Sergnese p. 92(cl), Alamy/Superstock p. 92(cr), Alamy/Willtung/Stockimo p. 93(bl); **Getty Images** pp. 25(bm), 28, Getty Images/Ascent Xmedia GmbH p. 30, Getty Images/Alexey Avdeev pp. 56–57, Getty Images/BigJoker p. 165(tape), Getty Images/CreativaImages pp. 40–41, Getty Images/DRB Images, LLC p. 26, Getty Images/Stephan Hoerold p. 58(br), Getty Images/JB Lacroix p. 47, Getty Images/Lokibaho p. 93(tr), Getty Images/Nicolas McComber p. 117, Getty Images/Nipitphon Na Chiangmai p. 127(br), Getty Images/PeopleImages pp. 25(br), 29, Getty Images/Ni Qin p. 164(bag), Getty Images/Roman Samokhin p. 162(can), Getty Images/Miguel Sotomayor p. 115, Getty Images/SSPL p. 127(tl), Getty Images/Karen Su p. 91(tr); **Nancy Judd** pp. 162–165; **Shutterstock** pp. 88–89, Shutterstock/Algor7 p. 91(bl), Shutterstock/cdrw pp. 120–121, Shutterstock/Gearstd pp. 58–59(background), 60–61(background), Shutterstock/Luc Kohnrn p. 60, Shutterstock/Stephanus Le Roux pp. 25(bl), 27, Shutterstock/Mirtmirt pp. 74–77, Shutterstock/Eduard Moldoveanu p. 58(tr), Shutterstock/Matyas Rehak p. 6, Shutterstock/Offset/Jasper James pp. 24–25, Shutterstock/Taigi pp. 4–7, 23, 39, 55, 71, 87, 103, 119, 135, 151, 167, Shutterstock/Zastolskiy Victor pp. 72–73.

Printed and bound in Dubai

2023 2022 2021 2020 2019
10 9 8 7 6 5